Songs in the Desert

To

Loretta,
my wife, lover, and friend
who has lived through too many deserts with me

and

Lance and Chad,
my sons, who love music as I do.
I am so proud of both of you!

Songs in the Desert

David Currie

SMYTH&HELWYS
PUBLISHING, INCORPORATED · MACON, GEORGIA

SMYTH&
HELWYS

Smyth & Helwys Publishing, Inc.
6316 Peake Road
Macon, Georgia 31210-3960
1-800-747-3016
©1999 by Smyth & Helwys Publishing
All rights reserved.
Printed in the United States of America.

David Currie

All biblical quotations are taken from the New Revised Standard
Version (NRSV) unless otherwise indicated.

Library of Congress Cataloging-in-Publication Data on file

ISBN 1-57312-258-0

Contents

Acknowledgments

I especially want to thank my staff, Charles McLaughlin and Charlotte Caffey, who faithfully read and reread each chapter, making corrections and invaluable suggestions. Charles is my first cousin and has been a fellow companion on my journey for many years. Charlotte has been my friend since she stood with me through one of my darkest deserts. Tricia Patterson, a new friend, did a valuable editing job for which I am grateful.

I would have accomplished little in my life without the loving friendship of Phil Strickland. I have never been in a desert where he abandoned me. Other special friends for many years are Gary Elliston, Jim Heerwald, Sam McCutchen, David Sapp, Doug Ezell, and Ira Peak. Any of them would take a call at 2 AM and be at my side the next day if I needed them. I am a lucky man to have such friends.

In the book I brag often on my mother. She is a jewel. My sister Carolyn and her family have always given me unconditional love and support. I am honored to be a part of this family.

A special thanks to the members and supporters of Texas Baptists Committed. They inspire me with their tireless support of Christ and religious freedom. They are my extended family in the faith. I am proud to work with them.

Introduction

I suppose the idea for this book is original. I know ministers often use popular songs as sermon illustrations, but I am not aware of anyone writing a book that combines the Bible and popular music as the main texts. If so, it is the only original thing I am contributing to the book. God wrote the Bible, the songwriters wrote the songs, and I borrowed the insights from the wonderful mentors, counselors, and friends who have been blessings to me.

The book is personal in many ways. It comes out of my life, my struggles, and the comfort and assistance I have found in music and the Bible. It could be more personal. I did not share details of the many times I have been on a dark, desert highway. I did not want the book to be about me. My prayer is that as you read the book, the songs, Scriptures, and stories will touch you and involve you in the deserts of your life and that you will find strength and comfort.

Life for me has often been a struggle. I have always had to battle my innate desire to be selfish, egotistical, materialistic, mean, despondent, and on and on. In short, I am human and often have denied my spiritual nature. Yet, I love being alive!

I am also a person of faith, a follower of Jesus Christ with whom I believe I have a personal relationship. I try to allow my faith to impact every area of my life. At times my relationship with Christ has been special and progressing. At other times my relationship with Christ has been stagnant and distant as I did not invest energy and time in the relationship.

Through the struggles of life and the times of great love and joy, I have listened to music and been affected emotionally by music. Singer/songwriter Amy Grant said it well: "To me, the real mystery of music is that it connects us to people, to an understanding, to a feeling, or to some kind of truth." I agree.

I want to clarify something at the beginning. This book refers to song lyrics from various writers and artists. I know none of these artists personally and have no idea if any of the songs I mention have any religious meaning at all to the persons who wrote or performed them. I do not know if any of these writers and performers are Christians (except Amy Grant who has publicly said she is a Christian). My guess is that none of these songs was written with a religious intent in mind. I simply do not know, and it would be inappropriate for me to try to speculate.

The fact is, "I hear" a certain message in these songs, even if the writers did not intend for me to. The songs speak to me because of who I am, not because the writers wrote them to convey a specific message I have somehow understood. Bob Dylan talked about this subject as he began a major tour in the fall of 1997. He said:

> You can't interpret a Hank Williams song. He's done the interpretation and the performance, and that's it. Now it's for the listener to decide if it moves him or not. That's something you don't even decide. That happens to you unconsciously. I let the songs fly, and people respond. Whether they make a valid interpretation or look at it with a false eye, I'm not concerned with that.

I may or may not be making a valid interpretation of the intentions of the songwriters. I have no way of knowing. These writers have thrown these lyrics out, and I have applied the meaning I heard in the songs in the midst of my joys and struggles.

A good example is the song that inspired the title of this book. It is an Eagles song, "Hotel California." I seriously doubt the Eagles had any religious intent in this song. In truth, I don't hear any either. But a couple of lyrics spoke to me and provided me with ideas for this book. The lyrics, "On a dark, desert highway . . .," did it for me. I began to think of life's struggles as being deserts. Nobody likes being trapped in a desert.

Scott Peck begins his famous book, *The Road Less Traveled*, with this sentence: "Life is difficult." When we are honest, life is difficult. And, when life has been its most difficult, I have found comfort from the Bible, my faith, and music. Unfortunately, I have found nothing that keeps me out of the deserts of life all the time. I do not believe it is possible to avoid the dark deserts of life, but we can survive them and even benefit from them.

Even faith in Christ will not keep us from the deserts of life. Believing in Jesus does not remove us from life's struggles, isolate us from life's disappointments, or keep us from the dark, desert highways. Believing in Jesus does not make us perfect people. Faith does not keep us from ending up in the deserts of life, "prisoners here of our own device," as the Eagles sing in another lyric from "Hotel California." Sometimes we make bad choices. Sometimes life just deals us a cruel blow. Whatever the reason, it has always been a struggle for me to make sense out of all of life's complexities—work, relationships, family, politics, religion. Many times I have found myself trying to survive the "dark, desert highway" of life. Making sense of life is perhaps a struggle for everyone, if they are honest about it. The realistic goals are survival and hopefully growth.

The spring of 1991 was a specially difficult dark, desert highway for me. Some relationships seemed, and were, too broken to fix. My career was at a stage of confusion. Not only did I not know the answers, but I also did not know the questions. Some of the questions I was asking then are still not answered today.

Life was a matter of survival. The pain I felt inside was so intense that I was reduced to living in 15-minute increments. I know people speak of living "one day at a time," but that seemed like eternity to me. I would just set a goal to make it for the next 15 minutes and take it from there.

A close friend, Doug Ezell, who had taught me in seminary and now is a family therapist, encouraged me "to live in

Psalms." He said the book of Psalms contains nearly all of our human emotions—anger, guilt, confusion, pain, questioning, abandonment, rejection, pride, love, and fear. I read Psalms as much as I could, underlining in red all the verses that spoke of God as being my savior or rock of strength or that spoke of feeling abandoned, alone, and afraid. I underlined a lot.

Life was difficult. I prayed a lot. I wrote prayers to God. I tried, as much as the pain would permit, to examine myself, to face my own private deserts. As much as possible, I tried to open my life to God. And, as throughout my life, I listened to music. I have always loved music, especially lyrics that capture human emotions in words.

I believe that God actively works to communicate His love through movies, music, art, and literature. Often I wonder if the writers are even aware that God is influencing them, but I believe He is.

Who could watch the movies *Schindler's List, Braveheart, Dead Man Walking,* or the incredible *Dead Poets Society* and not sense God at work?

Or who could hear Willie Nelson sing "The last thing I needed the first thing this morning was to have you walk out on me," or David Ball's "When the Thought of You Catches Up with Me," and not understand those emotions if they have experienced much of life at all? And when I hear George Jones sing "He Stopped Loving Her Today," the world stands still for three minutes. I believe God can use music to communicate with us.

A song that particularly spoke to me from 1990 to 1991 was Pam Tillis' "It's Just One of Those Things I Can't Do Nothing About." That is one of life's most difficult lessons to learn: you just can't fix some things no matter how hard you try. I was nearly 40 years old when that truth finally became a part of my life. As important a truth as it was to learn, it is still painful, and some days I still wish it were not so.

As far as literature dealing with the human condition and challenging us to think about our lives, Shakespeare wrote about it better than anyone. Frederick Buechner, Robert Farrar Capon, and Wendell Berry are my three favorite modern writers. They write masterfully, and their words touch my soul deeply.

In the spring of 1991 I drove to Austin, Texas, which took about four hours. I arrived a little early and stopped at a mall. I went to a music store and purchased some classic 70s rock cassettes. When I started my drive home, an idea came to mind. I was really comforted by the music. It touched many of my deepest emotions, just as the Psalms had touched my soul. The prayers I had written had also been very helpful. I started to listen with the idea of picking some songs out to make my own "comfort tape."

When I arrived home about 11 PM, I started to make my tape. In the introduction to the tape I said: "Psalms, songs, and prayers that were comforting to me during this very diffi- cult time in my life." Then I started to record the songs as I had arranged them in my mind. I would read the verses in Psalms I had underlined in red, without stopping between chapters or verses. Then I would record a song I had picked out, then start back in Psalms. Occasionally, I would read one of my prayers. It took about three hours to make my "comfort tape." The combination of music, psalms, and prayers seemed to comfort others as much as it did me. A part of comfort is actually letting yourself feel the emotion so that healing can occur. That is one of the ways God can use music to help us in the deserts of life.

A February 1997 episode of a TV show conveyed this truth. The main star met a famous musician and said, "I love your music. I listen to it when I'm depressed." The singer replied, "I hope it makes you feel better." The main actor answered, "No, it makes me feel worse." This dialogue conveys the truth that healing cannot occur unless our inner pain is brought to the surface, stared in the face, and dealt with. Music can bring thoughts and feelings to our consciousness that we need to get out into the open. That is what music has done for me through the years—brought up emotions and prompted thoughts I needed to deal with in my life. I believe it does that for others, too, and that is why so many of us love music.

The thesis of this book could easily come from the Eagles song "Learn To Be Still." According to the lyrics, we are like sheep without a shepherd, wandering into the deserts of life and often following the wrong gods home. The desert is hot and uncomfortable. It can be especially scary if we are alone. When we are in the deserts of life, it is easy to trust the wrong gods, go in the wrong direction, and make the wrong decisions.

This book is also about God and how He wants to help us in the midst of and off the dark, desert highway. As a Christian, I believe the ultimate reason for existence is to share one's life with God and be a partner with His work and redemptive ministry in the world. I hope this book helps persons caught in the deserts of life to open themselves to God and God's power to comfort and transform their lives along the journey of life.

The intent of this book is to comfort and challenge. Sometimes we do end up in the desert because of our own choices. We must address this reality if we are to learn from our struggles. I will seek to challenge us regarding our bad choices while remembering we need comfort even then. Sometimes life just knocks us down, and we must simply survive those deserts.

The deserts of life are real for each of us. To be honest, I do not believe any of us can completely avoid the deserts of life. We all have demons and desires. Human beings simply have too many problems. Even strong Christians struggle with demons inside themselves. Every person, if they are honest, spends much of their life in some kind of desert. We all have a dark side, and persons who hide it behind their piety may be in the darkest desert of all.

My conviction is that I have survived and am surviving the deserts of life with the help of God and God's Word. In many instances music has helped me by prompting me to feel my pain, thus allowing healing. For me, many songs prophetically deal with the human condition. They deal with broken hearts, of course, but also deal with trying to fill the emptiness many experience, materialism, dangers of pride and anger, living as a victim, and the struggle to understand freedom. Many songs deal with the deserts we all experience because of our humanity. When we are in the desert the experience may feel like hell, but the possibility exists for the event to end up being heavenly. Let me explain.

Nat Tracy was in his 60s when I walked into Old Testament class for the first time as an 18-year-old college freshman. The first day of class he told us, "No matter how much you think of yourself, it is not as much as God does." I have never forgotten hearing him say those words. I went on to take his classes for eight straight semesters, every course he taught. He made the gospel come alive for me. He told me of a God who loves me unconditionally—no ifs, ands, or buts. He told me that being a disciple does not mean being a perfect person, but rather being a "willing learner," "a teachable person," someone who tries to cooperate with God in using all of life's experiences to make himself more Christlike.

I remember one specific illustration Nat Tracy gave. Partnering with God is like a man who makes a Persian rug but messes up his pattern. So, when he gets to the opposite side of the rug, he puts the same mistake there, and the rug ends up being more beautiful than it would have originally been. Dr. Tracy said that's what God can do in our lives if we let Him. God can take our mistakes and pain and use them to make us more beautiful in character than we would have been without the experiences, even when we end up in the desert because of our own choices. In essence, the dark deserts can be heaven or hell. My hope for this book is that it helps you make those deserts heavenly—or at least more survivable.

Chapter 1

The Desert of Broken Relationships

Pretend you have never heard of country music. Pretend you have a friend who is always talking about how wonderful country music is. Ask him to play one song that best captures the essence of country music. If I were the friend, I would play "He Stopped Loving Her Today" by George Jones. There are thousands of songs that deal with the theme of broken relationships, but this is the classic.

To me, country music—really all good music—speaks to our hearts and touches our deepest emotions. I recall David Allen Coe's song about Hank Williams, which has the lyrics, "Boy, can you make folks feel what you feel inside?" A great song makes the listener feel what the songwriter felt when he or she wrote the song, or even better, opens you up to "feel what you feel inside."

Broken relationships hurt badly and for a long time. They can leave scars that may never heal, especially if we never give them a chance to heal. For the man in the song, the pain finally stopped when he died and "stopped loving her." Are you still dealing with the pain of a broken relationship?

Mark and Susan were high school sweethearts. They married before their senior year of college. They had three beautiful children ages 17, 15, and 11. They had been married 19 years when it happened. Susan simply left, saying she didn't know who she was anymore. She left Mark. She left her children. She left her job and took another one in a city 200 miles away.

No one who knew Mark and Susan had a clue. They were active in church. Mark was a deacon and taught high school juniors. Susan worked in the six-year-old department. Their children sang in the youth choir and went to camp every summer. The family lived comfortably, able to afford a vacation each summer and a spring ski trip. They didn't entertain often. Susan was a private person and didn't enjoy socializing much, but they had friends. She and Mark appeared to be each other's best friend.

Obviously, something was wrong, but Mark claimed he had no idea. After Susan left, she would not even consider reconciliation. Six months late, she filed for divorce. She asked for nothing. She willingly agreed for Mark to have custody of the children, although she faithfully visited them one weekend a month. When she did come back, she visited the children in a motel, and she never saw any of her old friends. She never went back to church there. As Mark said over and over, "I can't tell you why." Susan never gave him any reasons.

Mark and Susan are fictional names of fictional people. Yet I know or have known some real-life situations very similar to theirs. You can probably think of persons who could be Mark or Susan. Maybe you can relate to one of them as you read their narrative. Maybe you have been Mark or Susan yourself.

The reality of life is that all of us experience broken relationships. Hopefully, we do not go through a divorce, but nearly 50 percent of Americans do. Hopefully, we do not have a broken relationship with our parents or with one of our children, but many of us do. We have had a very meaningful friendship that ended, and we never understood why. Each of us has experienced the most final of broken relationships—the death of someone we love.

The desert of broken relationships is something we all walk through. It is what you feel when driving through the desert and your car overheats, then breaks down. You have no water; the sun burns down; it's 112° in the shade; you are scared. Sometimes a broken relationship continues to prey upon your mind for years.

Jesus' disciples experienced this feeling. Imagine what they must have felt on Saturday morning, the day after Jesus' crucifixion. They had left families, jobs, and possessions for a relationship with the Messiah. They had bet that Jesus was someone special, but after only three years, he was dead. He had not even tried to keep from being killed. He wouldn't even defend himself at his trial. The disciples never thought they'd be alone. Surely they were scared. They could not go back, and the future was so uncertain.

All of the disciples except Judas—who, as Carlyle Marney said, "did not wait to see what God could do with what he had done"—were in for a major surprise. What looked so bad on Saturday changed radically on Sunday morning. Jesus had risen from the dead. He was alive! The despair of Saturday morning turned to tears of joy on Sunday morning.

One of the most important things to remember when we are in the desert of a broken relationship is that tomorrow is another day. What looks so bad now may look totally different in only a little while. It is the survival that hurts while waiting for tomorrow to come.

The Bible is a book about relationships. First, it speaks of how to live in relationship with God. It also speaks of how to live in proper relationship with other people and with nature. It is full of stories of relationships, beginning with Adam and Eve, and never stops. In the New Testament even the letters Paul wrote to churches are about his relationship with those churches and the people in them. The entire Bible is about relationships. Since they are human relationships, few of them go very smoothly. All have their share of tension.

Many of the stories in the Bible describe broken relationships. Adam and Eve broke their relationship with God. Their story is symbolic of how all of us have a broken relationship with God and how God seeks reconciliation. Abraham and Lot parted ways early on in their journey. Hosea and Gomer certainly had an on-again/off-again relationship that symbolized the relationship between God and His chosen people. Samson and Delilah had a torrid love affair that ended in betrayal. Even Paul and Barnabas argued over who should accompany them on their missionary journeys, so they parted company. The biblical story of David and Jonathan describes a friendship that ended sadly.

Jonathan was the son of King Saul. Twelve-year-old David, after killing Goliath, was chosen to replace Saul as king of Israel. David and Jonathan were best friends. Jonathan's Dad, King Saul, sought to kill David because he was jealous of David's popularity and David's having been chosen to succeed him as king. David and Jonathan made some promises to each other regarding their friendship. David had to defend himself against the armies of King Saul. Jonathan saved David's life from his father, Saul. Ultimately, Saul and Jonathan were killed in the same battle.

David lost a friend. It was painful. The Bible records in 2 Samuel 1 David's lament over Saul and Jonathan. David wrote, "I grieve for you, Jonathan my brother; you were very dear to me. Your love for me was wonderful, more wonderful than that of women." What moving words of friendship!

Despite his sadness, David went on to do great things. The Bible describes him as "a man after God's own heart." Pain did not defeat him. To be honest, David also went on to do many stupid things. No soap opera could ever improve on David's relationships. From Jonathan, to his own children who betrayed him, to his affair with Bathsheba and having her husband killed—this is real human stuff that would make the front page of today's newspapers. No wonder the psalms, mostly written by David, record human emotions so well. David experienced them all.

One of the saddest pictures in life is that of a person who has stopped living and is simply existing. The song "He Stopped Loving Her Today" describes such a person. The lyrics say, "He kept her picture on the wall, went half crazy now and then," but he continued to love her and hope she would return.

Many people stop living the day of the funeral or the day the divorce is final. For some, the pain of the loss is so intense they are never willing or able to work through it. They never entertain the possibility that the future might be better than the past. They can't stop wondering what they left behind or longing for what might have been. Therefore, they are not open to what good thing could be a part of their life at present.

Some broken relationships are extremely painful. I have been there more than I care to remember. It is tempting to spend time, as the band Little Texas sang, thinking about "What Might Have Been." When I hear that song, it takes me back to a couple of specific memories: my first serious girlfriend as a senior in high school and a woman I knew who had a large ranch and walls around her that reached to the sky. I like the feeling, the nostalgia. I feel the same emotions when I hear Dan Fogelberg's "Another Old Lang Syne" that speaks about a man running into his old girlfriend in the grocery store. I will always love Harry Chapin's song, "Taxi," about the cab driver who wants to be a pilot and picks up his former girlfriend and carries her to her mansion where she lives a lonely life. I smile when I hear those songs. Although they touch my soul deeply, I don't live there anymore.

Yet, the temptation to live in the past challenges us all. It is often easier to live in the past because it is less painful than the present. It takes work and discipline to fight through the pain toward wholeness. The problem is that by dwelling on what used to be, on what was left behind, God and others can't be active in our lives in the present. No matter how deep the pain, this is never the way to deal with a broken relationship. Mark or Susan or the kids could get stuck giving their hearts to the past.

Another bad option is to live in denial, acting as if the broken relationship is not painful. In our case study Mark could act as if Susan's leaving did not bother him. He could block out his feelings. He could ignore his pain. But the result would be as bad as living in the past. He must face his pain, place it in the open so it can run the course of healing. Ignoring the pain simply leaves it under the surface, which will affect all his future relationships.

Another bad option for dealing with a broken relationship is to stop at the anger stage. Anger is a normal stage of grief, but some people remain so angry over their broken relationship—angry at God or their former spouse, employer, or child—that it dominates their lives and continues to affect all their relationships. It is a dangerous desert to be stuck in. It accomplishes nothing and eats at the soul.

Joe Cocker and Jennifer Warren sang a song titled "Up Where We Belong." It was part of the soundtrack of the movie, *An Officer and a Gentleman*. It talks about hanging on to the past and always looking behind, whereas all we have is the here and now. One of my favorite songs is "This Night Won't Last Forever," written by Bill LaBounty and Roy Freeland and performed by Sawyer Brown. The lyrics convey hope for a bright tomorrow and the knowledge that a broken heart will mend. Both of these songs typify the attitude a

Christian should have, even in the darkest desert. We believe in a God of second chances, a God who took the disciples' despair on Friday night and turned it to joy on Sunday morning. The lyrics challenge us to look ahead, to be open to the future being better than the past. They remind us that time does heal wounds if we will allow.

Clint Black sings a song about leaving a relationship a "better man." The song reminds us that each experience provides an opportunity for knowledge and personal growth, no matter how painful. In fact, the saying "no pain, no gain" is applicable. We learn the most from painful experiences. Pain lets us know something is wrong. Physically, pain alerts us to injury and the need to get help. The same principle applies in our emotional and spiritual lives. Pain lets us know we need to seek help from God and others.

People often feel that pain is the result of the wrath of God, of God punishing us. Dr. Nat Tracy helped me understand the wrath of God in a new way I found very meaningful. God's wrath is not God's anger. It is not to be understood as God being mad and paying people back for their sinful, stupid behavior. The wrath of God is simply the other side of God's love. When we live in harmony with God, we experience His love. When we live selfishly, out of harmony with God's teachings, we experience His wrath. It is a natural consequence, not God's intentional choice. The wrath of God is the natural result of disobedience. It is painful, and that is good. The pain tells us we are living in an unhealthy manner.

Dr. Tracy told us it is good that a hot stove burns. If it didn't, we would leave our hands on it until we were really injured. Since it is painful to touch a hot stove, we quickly pull our hands away and usually aren't injured badly. The heat of the stove protects us. It is good for us that it burns. A painful experience, a broken relationship, is not wasted time if we handle it in a healthy way. The way to handle it is to remember the definition of a disciple—to be a willing learner.

There is much to learn from all of life's experiences if we are open. One thing to learn is the role we played in bringing about the broken relationship. In our fictional story Mark could easily blame his broken marriage on Susan. After all, she is the one who left him and their children. Worst of all, she never gave a reason.

Mark won't learn much that way, however. Is there such a thing as an innocent party in a broken relationship? All of us are far beyond innocence. Selfishness, or biblically speaking, sinfulness, is a part of all of us. Mark played a role in his broken relationship. He needs to take the time necessary and do the work required to understand his contribution. Otherwise, he could view himself as a victim all his life.

To get on with his life, Mark also needs to work through his grief over the broken relationship. His life did not end with his divorce. He still has children who need to know and experience his love and care. God is also a God of second (and third and fiftieth) chances. Mark needs to use his time wisely working through the pain, anger, and sorrow in order to be healthy enough to have another opportunity at love.

The Bible describes Jesus as "a man of sorrows, acquainted with grief." We all are. The most painful grief we usually encounter is some form of a broken relationship. The Bible is the story of God's attempt to bring all persons back into His family. God desires a relationship with every person. He is the one who seeks us, like He did with Adam and Eve. Everyone can have a relationship with God by simply opening themselves to the reality of their need for such a relationship and participating in it.

In the midst of the desert of a broken relationship, remember that "this night won't last forever." The end of a special relationship, no matter how precious, is not the end of life. It does not have to be permanent reality, not with the Creator of the universe as our friend, teacher, and life partner who never leaves.

Chapter 2

The Desert of Deception

"Lyin' Eyes" is an awesome song by my favorite musical group, the Eagles. I do not know what the Eagles had in mind when they wrote it, but as I listen to it, I hear an intriguing, sad story. I hear a song that is about a temptation we are all too familiar with—the human temptation to live a lie, to pretend to be something or someone we are not. It is a desert we all experience because facing the truth about events, ourselves, and our own actions can be truly painful.

The woman in the song "Lyin' Eyes" is living in the desert of deception. She deceives herself into believing security and money can make her happy. She marries a "rich, old man" she doesn't love. She may not have to worry about money, but she despises giving her love to "a man with hands as cold as ice."

Her first mistake was deceiving herself. She married for money, to meet her need for security and possessions, and then found that those needs were not really important to her. We have all known people who made choices based on money, fame, security, or their parents' wishes only later to regret their decisions. Perhaps we, too, have made such decisions.

After she stops deceiving herself and realizes her deeper need for love, she makes another bad choice. Rather than deal with her current situation first, she opts for more deception. Rather than tell her husband the truth, getting a divorce and not taking any of his money, she finds a younger man to be her lover. She sneaks to the other side of town to be with him.

By the end of "Lyin' Eyes," the woman seems to think in a healthier manner. At least she is facing her deceptive life enough to ask herself "how it ever got this crazy." She is going through the painful process of admitting she feels "like a fool." She faces the fact that she got what she thought she wanted only to find it wasn't what she wanted, that her new life "didn't change things." She deceived herself about who she really was and what her real needs were and paid a terrible price.

The deepest need we have is to be known and loved by another, especially God. When we seek to meet lesser needs, we end up with the same old empty spot in the pit of our stomachs. I think that is what the Eagles were singing about in "After the Thrill Is Gone." The lyrics say that love is not a feeling, but a passion, a commitment of oneself to another.

The Bible is full of stories about deception and people seeking to be loved and blessed. One of the most interesting stories is that of Jacob. (In Hebrew the name Jacob translates to "deceiver.") Jacob learned the art of deception early. In Hebrew tradition the blessing and inheritance of the father went to the oldest son. Jacob had an older brother Esau, whom his father Isaac loved. Esau was a "man's man" as we would say, a hunter, a man of the open country. Esau was a big, burly, hairy man. Jacob was fair and smooth-skinned. Rebekah, the boy's mother, preferred Jacob. She wanted Jacob to have the blessing, so she helped him with a plan to help him steal it.

It is a fascinating story in Genesis 25–27. Isaac is almost blind and about to die. He realizes it is time to give the blessing, to pass on his inheritance, to Esau. He sends Esau away on a hunting trip to bring him some of his favorite wild game. Isaac tells Esau to come back and prepare the meat for him the way he likes it. Isaac promises to convey to Esau his blessing after the meal.

Rebekah overhears Isaac's instructions to Esau. Since she wants the blessing to go to Jacob, she starts to implement her plan of deception. She tells Jacob to get a young goat, and she will prepare it as Isaac likes. Then she helps Jacob cover his smooth hands and neck with goatskins, so he will feel like Esau when Isaac touches him. Jacob takes the meat to Isaac and claims to be Esau. Isaac touches his son and, feeling the hairy arms, believes it is Esau, although the voice is Jacob's. He gives the blessing to Jacob.

The interesting twist to the story for the rest of us who wander into the desert of deception is that Jacob is a major character in the Old Testament, much more so than Esau. Despite the deception, God blesses and uses Jacob in mighty ways. God makes Jacob the same promises he made Abraham. God told Jacob, "I am with you and will watch over you wherever you go." The story offers the rest of us deceivers hope for the future.

Another story of deception in the Bible worth noting is the story in Matthew 26 of Peter when he denied he was a follower of Christ. Jesus tells Peter he will deny him three times. Peter, impulsive and emotional, strongly protests that he will never do such a thing. In fact, Peter says, "Even if I have to die, I will never disown you." Shortly thereafter, when Jesus is taken into custody by the authorities, Peter is identified as a follower of Jesus. He denies the charge. Later he denies that he even knows Jesus, much less is a follower. Finally, he denies his relationship with Christ a third time, just as Jesus had told him he would.

We have an innate capacity to be deceivers. We are deceptive to ourselves, to others, and to God. The result of leading a life of deception is that it affects all our relationships—with ourselves, with others, and with God. It is hard to live a lie.

Jacob grew up in the desert of deception. Peter wandered into the desert of deception alone and afraid. There is a way out of the desert of deception—for Jacob, Peter, the girl in "Lyin' Eyes," and each of us. It is not painless or easy. It takes courage, but it is not complicated. The way out of the desert of deception is to be honest with ourselves, others, and God.

Wendell Berry describes the process beautifully in his short story, "The Wild Birds." In this story Burley Coulter goes to his cousin, Wheeler, who is an attorney, to make out his will. Burley, who has never married, takes his nephew Nathan with him. Burley, who Wheeler expects will leave his farm to Nathan, tells Wheeler he is leaving his farm to Danny Branch. Wheeler tries to talk Burley out of it, but he will have none of it. Burley believes Danny is his son. He has never acknowledged this before, though most of the small town figures it is so. Burley has decided to leave the desert of deception. What he says is a lesson for us.

> If Nathan needed what I've got, I'd have to think of that. He don't. Besides what he has got on his own, he's his daddy's heir, and in the right way. You might say that he has come, as far as he has got anyhow, by the main road, the way you have, Wheeler, and has been regular. I haven't been regular. I've come by a kind of back path—through the woods, you might say, and along the bluffs. Whatever I've come to, I've mostly got there too late, and mostly by surprise.
>
> I don't say everybody *has* to be regular. Being out of regular may be all right—I liked it mostly. It may be in your nature. Maybe it's even useful in a way. But it finally gets to be a question of what you can recommend. . . . Your

way has been different from mine, but by my way I've come here where you are, and now I've got to know it and act like it. I know you can't make the irregular regular, but when you have rambled out of sight, you have to come back into the clear and show yourself.[1]

The road out of the desert of deception is to come back in the clear and stop living the lie. Come clean. Face the music. Tell the truth. It is not an easy course to take, but it is the only course out of the desert of deception.

First, you've got to tell yourself the truth. You have to ask yourself "how it ever got this crazy." You have to admit "you feel like a fool." You have to take responsibility for your own actions. Sure, your parents could have raised you better. Maybe you only knew one parent. Sure, you wish you hadn't been raised in a broken home. Sure, you wish you had been born smarter, richer, better looking. Your choices still have been your choices. The buck stopped with you.

Burley Coulter told himself the truth, the truth he had always known but did not want to acknowledge, even to himself. Burley faced the truth and admitted the deception. Peter did the same thing. The setting for Peter's denial of Christ was just prior to Christ's crucifixion. Jesus had been arrested and questioned by the religious authorities. Peter had been with him when he was arrested and had responded with anger, even cutting off the ear of a soldier. Within hours, Peter denied even knowing Christ. After denying Christ three times, he "went outside and wept bitterly." Like Burley Coulter, Peter faced the truth and admitted his deception.

The second step out of deception is being honest with others. By this I mean honestly facing what the deception is doing to those around you—your spouse, your children, your partner in deception, those who love and value you. I do not mean you should admit everything to everyone like an open book. That may or may not be healthy. I know people who feel it is necessary to air out all their "dirty laundry" only to make themselves feel better and everyone else feel worse.

Burly had to admit what his deception would mean to Danny Branch. Danny would have missed both his inheritance and the joy of being claimed. In essence, Burley was giving Danny his blessing. Burley was saying to Danny, "You are my son, and I am proud of you." Danny had a right to know the truth and not be punished anymore by Burley's deception.

The final step out of deception is being honest with God. Being deceptive does not just hurt you and other people; it hurts God and His kingdom. You need to seek and accept the forgiveness of God. Everyone is a sinner, a deceiver. Everyone hurts other people and themselves. Every biblical character, except Jesus, was a moral failure. The real character of anyone is not revealed in their goodness, since none of us is truly good, nor in their superior morality, since none of us is always moral, but in how they deal with their mistakes. Remember, the main characteristic of a disciple is not morality or perfection, but the attitude of a "willing learner," a teachable person. If Jesus had selected his disciples based on their morality keeping the law, he would have chosen Pharisees rather than zealots, tax-collectors, and fishermen.

Peter denied Christ three times. Was his career over? Was he forever viewed as a failure? Did God give up on him and write him off as a moral degenerate? I do not think so. The book of Acts describes this master of deception as a powerful preacher in the first-century church. I pray we all can move from our deserts of deception with lessons having been learned and sincerely seek to be used of God to help others. Don't try to live your life in the desert of deception, and you and those around you will be much happier.

Note

[1]Wendell Berry, "The Wild Birds," in *The Wild Birds* (San Francisco: North Point Press, 1986) 134-35.

Chapter 3

The Desert of Isolation

Pat was a beautiful woman, even in her early 50s. She was bright, one of the top attorneys in the city. She was popular at her firm, respected in the community, and served on several major committees in her church. Larry loved Pat deeply. He wasn't sure what part of her he loved the most—her mind, her spirit, or her physical beauty. He guessed he just loved all of her. He wanted to marry her more than anything else in his life, but he knew he shouldn't.

He had dated Pat for more than two years. She would be a good financial partner since Pat was very successful. She would be a good vacation partner since Pat loved to travel. They

would have years of stimulating intellectual and political dis-
cussions since Pat loved to examine and argue about major
issues in society. But Larry knew he wouldn't have a wife, a
real partner, because he could not get close to Pat. Every time
he heard the song, "The Rose," Larry thought of Pat. The
lyrics described her perfectly.

> It's the heart afraid of breaking, that never learns to dance;
> It's the dream afraid of waking, that never takes a chance.

Pat would not take chances, and she was afraid of being hurt.

Larry kept trying to build an intimate relationship with
Pat, but whenever he tried to steer their conversation toward
deep, personal feelings, Pat emotionally distanced herself. She
would not open herself to anyone. Three earlier marriages had
ended in divorce. She did not want to take that chance again.
The second marriage had been especially painful. She had
rushed into it, feeling lonely and afraid, and it had been a dis-
aster. Her husband had become mentally and physically
abusive. In her opinion the risks were simply too great. Being
vulnerable meant being hurt as far as Pat was concerned. The
upside was not worth the risk. She'd been down that road
before.

Larry had known people who built walls around their
heart to protect themselves, but Pat had built a fortress with a
moat full of alligators. He would sadly laugh to himself that he
"could climb walls, but Pat's walls went to the sky." Finally, the
relationship ended. Larry moved on with his life and married
someone else. He often thanked God that Pat had resisted his
desires. Pat married a rich, older man. She passed on love and
took security. In truth, it was the best she could do, given
where she was in her life.

The desert of isolation is a terribly lonely place. I do not
believe anyone chooses to go there without having experienced
a great deal of emotional pain. Still, staying there is not
healthy. It is not the place to be if you want to experience life

at its fullest and best. Of course, someone in the desert of isolation doesn't believe life can be very joyous and full. Perhaps
they feel they went for the best life has to offer in some prior
relationship and found it pretty lousy.

First, a positive word about one form of isolation. Being
alone can be healthy. It is important to be so comfortable with
yourself that you enjoy your own company. It is important to
know yourself. It is often important to isolate yourself with
God. Jesus often went away to be alone, to pray, to be
renewed. Before he started his ministry, he prayed and fasted
for 40 days. This gave him the strength to resist the three
temptations the devil gave him in the desert.

Everyone needs a day of rest. All work and no play is not
healthy. Mature people like themselves, are comfortable being
alone, and do not make decisions simply out of their needs
and emotions. Being isolationist, insofar as feeling comfortable
spending time alone and not acting out of weakness, is a positive trait. But there is a very destructive and unhealthy side to
isolationism. It is this kind of isolation the song "The Rose"
describes. This song speaks of a person afraid to love, to be
open, to risk, to be vulnerable. Life for her is closed. She is
afraid to dance, to take a chance, to give of herself, and
ultimately to live.

People in the desert of isolation are hard people to get
close to. Therefore, they risk missing life's most beautiful gifts
—meaningful relationships with God and others. Because of
the possibility of pain, isolated people never risk the possibility
of love and joy. They can't handle the good and the bad as
important aspects of life.

Jesus understood that all of life is a mixture of good and
bad and of the dangers of practicing isolation. The parable of
the tares or weeds that Jesus tells in Matthew 13 speaks to me
of the desert of isolation. It is the story of a farmer who sows
good wheat seed in his field only to have his enemy, while
everyone is asleep, sow the same field with weeds. The wheat
and the weeds come up together. The farmer's workers offer to

pull up the weeds, but the farmer, being very wise, replies, "No, because while you are pulling the weeds, you may root up the wheat with them. Let them grow together until the harvest" (vv. 29-30).

There is true wisdom in this parable. Life is always a bittersweet reality. Few, if any, experiences or relationships are all good or all bad. The problem with isolating ourselves against the bad is that in doing so, we also isolate ourselves against the good. And that is too great a price to pay.

Frederick Buechner wrote that someone once told him he had been "a good steward of his pain." He reflected on his life and admitted that his writing gifts may have, in many ways, developed out of his own life's journey to deal with personal pain and his willingness to be open to it and learn from it.

Buechner shares this truth beautifully in a section of his autobiography entitled, *The Sacred Journey*. His father committed suicide when Buechner was nine years old. His mother decided to take him and his brother and move to Bermuda. His grandmother Scharmann, did not approve of this move and told the family so strongly. Read the truths Buechner shares about the desert of isolation.

> "You should stay and face reality," she [Scharmann] wrote, and in terms of what was humanly best, this was perhaps the soundest advice she could have given us; that we should stay and, through sheer Scharmann endurance, will, courage, put our lives back together by becoming as strong as she was herself. But when it comes to putting broken lives back together—when it comes, in religious terms, to the saving of souls—the human best tends to be at odds with the holy best. To do for yourself the best that you have it in you to do—to grit your teeth and clench your fists in order to survive the world at its harshest and worst—is, by that very act, to be unable to let something be done for you and in you that is more wonderful still. The trouble with steeling yourself against the harshness of reality is that the same steel that secures your life against being destroyed

secures your life also against being opened up and transformed by the holy power that life itself comes from. You can survive on you own. You can grow strong on your own. You can even prevail on your own. But you cannot become human on your own . . . the one thing a clenched fist cannot do is accept a helping hand.[1]

Buechner seems to understand human emotions deeply. He is an ordained minister whose ministry has been writing novels and other books. I especially like the four novels he wrote about Leo Bibb. The novels are not specifically religious in nature but speak to the heart and mind in profound ways. The characters have real flaws and yet struggle with living their faith. Buechner strongly believes that God is always trying to speak to us through our lives. God cannot reach us when we are locked in the desert of isolation.

Other authors have also written on the danger of living life in isolation. Scott Peck, in his book, *The Road Less Traveled*, comments on the necessity of risking deep loss in order to achieve happiness in life:

There is always the risk of loss or rejection. If you move out to another human being, there is always the risk that that person will move away from you, leaving you more painfully alone than you were before. Love anything that lives— a person, a pet, a plant—and it will die. Trust anybody and you may be hurt; depend on anyone and that one may let you down. If someone is determined not to risk pain, then such a person must do without . . . all that makes life alive, meaningful, and significant.[2]

The desert of isolation is not a place to experience life at its fullest. Sometimes it may be a place one has to go for awhile to survive the harshness of life at the moment, but it is not a place to build a home and take up permanent residence. The home will be a lonely place. There will be little light, little excitement, and little joy.

Isolationists "never learn to dance." The pain of life stays locked away, buried, ignored. Thus, healing never occurs. Without healing, we never fully experience the wonderful emotions of life. As the song says, persons in the desert of isolation never cry, smile, or laugh like someone truly involved with love and life. They have made themselves untouchable. They walk through life alone. They may have relationships, but they are always relationships that can be controlled. If isolationists find themselves experiencing emotions they can't control, they run. The risks are too great.

Isolationists need to hear and believe the last verse of "The Rose." They need to remember that winter turns to spring, that the dead-looking trees in January come alive in April, that the brown grass of February gives way to the green grass of May. They need to remember that they can come alive again, no matter how tragic life has been or how deeply they have been hurt.

If you are stranded in the desert of isolation, I know you have your reasons. I know it is scary to open up your heart. I know the risks are great. Despite the potential pain, I believe the risks are worth it. I believe life in the desert of isolation truly means one is missing all that makes life alive, meaningful, and significant. With the Son's love, you, too, can become as beautiful as a rose.

Note

[1]Frederick Buechner, *The Sacred Journey* (San Francisco: Harper & Row, 1982) 46.

[2]M. Scott Peck, *The Road Less Traveled: A New Psychology of Love, Traditional Values, and Spiritual Growth* (New York: Touchstone Books, 1978) 132-33.

Chapter 4

The Desert of Shattered Dreams

"You have to live in the real world." If I have heard that statement once, I have heard it 500 times. It is one of my mother's favorite sayings. She usually reserves it for times when she thinks I have lost touch with reality, when I have let my dreams get the best of me. It is her way of telling me to "stay grounded; do not live in a fantasy world." She also uses it when I am feeling pain over something that has not gone the way I had hoped, whether it be in my work or with my family. At those times I especially do not like the phrase, although there is much truth to every word.

The problem with living in the real world is that reality hurts. The real world is often much more about coping with failure than celebrating success whether in personal relationships, family, or career.

Chase was born to be an athlete. Sports came easy to him. Name the sport, he could do it, and probably much better than you. He was good even when he didn't work at it. When he did work at it, he was great, great enough possibly to make a career of it. But Chase will never know for sure. His dreams were stolen.

Football was his sport of choice. He was one of those athletes who could play several positions equally well. In high school he was an all-state quarterback. He played in the Texas high school all-star game as a defensive back. He signed a scholarship with the same college where his father had played. He was converted to wide receiver. The future was bright. His dreams were coming true.

Chase dove for a pass the first week of fall practice. He landed on his shoulder. Something hurt badly. The shoulder had separated. He was out for the season. As a freshman, that was bearable. It was easier to concentrate on the tougher challenge of college academics. He could sit out a year—"redshirt" is the proper term—and still have four years to play. It would probably take him five years to graduate anyway.

Spring drills went well. He moved up the depth chart to second team as a redshirt freshman. Things were falling into place. He spent the summer in his small hometown where everybody treated him like a football hero. Being the football hero in a small Texas town makes you quite a celebrity. But just like with the professional superstars, it is easy to lose your perspective.

Chase returned to fall drills, and then it happened again. He dove for a pass; the shoulder was shot. The doctors said he could play again as long as he was willing to be operated on yearly. His season would always last only until the shoulder separated again. In reality, his career and his dreams were over.

The coaches were very honorable. They told him his scholarship, worth thousands of dollars, was still good. He could help the team as a student coach. But a haunting question ate at his soul: "Am I a failure?" His total identity was tied up in being a football star. The depression was difficult. He quit school and went home. The football hero became just another 19-year-old trying to figure out what to do with his life. It wasn't easy. It took him years to stop sitting at home evenings watching films of his high school games when he was the star and everyone cheered. He had no other dreams.

The only things certain in life are death and taxes, the saying goes. The other thing certain in life is that the unexpected should be expected. Pick up a newspaper any day of the week, and there will be story after story about shattered dreams. Some are simple tragedies. Others are failures of judgment. Many are about broken relationships. Some are dreams that didn't come true. Someone or some team will have won, and someone or some team will have lost.

"Here in the Real World" is a song about a shattered dream. The lyrics speak of how that in the movies "cowboys don't cry and heroes don't die," that if life were like the movies, "I'd never be blue." The song is grounded in reality. The sad truth is that many, if not most, of our dreams never come true; "the boy don't always get the girl, here in the real world."

Midlife crisis is the phrase we have coined for that time in middle age when someone realizes that most of their dreams did not come true and are not going to come true. They haven't been as successful as they had dreamed in many areas of their lives. They look back on the broken marriage, the missed promotions, the bad investments and wonder what might have been. "Here in the Real World" prompts me to think of what might have been, of how I would do many things differently if only I could.

There is something mystical, spiritual even, about sharing your dreams with fellow dreamers. I remember the wonderful friendship I had with Gary in college and continue to have today. Boy, did we ever dream of changing the world "with words like love and freedom." The debate was over who would be governor first. We would meet at an old church close to campus. We prayed together. We dreamed together. He went to law school; I went to seminary. He is a tremendous success, has his own firm in Dallas, and is still a very close friend. He has made a valuable contribution to society as an ethical lawyer with as much integrity as anyone I have ever known. In my efforts I hope I have made a contribution to religious liberty. Neither of us, I am quite sure, has any interest in being governor.

Our dreams were mostly ego-driven and foolish, despite their noble intentions. We definitely have not changed the world, but I think we are both very happy with where we are in life today. Hopefully, reality helped us live out more realistic dreams. A part of growing up is dreaming new dreams and letting go of past dreams.

I have many minister friends who were going to change the world only to find that the ministry is a lonely fishbowl and that their talents and/or God's will for them did not include becoming the next Billy Graham. In Texas there are more than 5,700 Baptist churches and missions. Only 750 of these average more than 250 people in attendance on a given Sunday morning. Most of the ministerial students I went to seminary with who dreamed of being the pastor of a large, influential congregation ended up being the pastor of a small, unknown congregation that struggles financially and spiritually to survive. Many of my peers are no longer in the ministry. It's not quite what they had planned or dreamed.

I know some people who invested their life savings in a new business only to file bankruptcy within months. I have friends in politics who lost elections and dropped from public view. I know people who got their dream job only to find that reality was a nightmare. The fact is, more dreams do not come true than do. Only one team wins the game. Only one person wins the contest.

The second aspect of shattered dreams has to do with dreams coming true, but not being fulfilling. "The Sad Cafe" by the Eagles questions "why fortune smiles on some and lets the rest go free."

Success has its price. It is the unsuccessful who go free. They do not have to carry the burden of success or bear the responsibility of extraordinary talent. Jesus said, "To whom much is given, much is required." Being talented and gifted can be a heavy responsibility. The public makes demands on the successful, and the successful make demands on themselves to live up to the success.

A good example is Alex Rodriguez, the shortstop for the Seattle Mariners, who hit .358 with 36 home runs as a 20-year-old in 1996. No right-handed batter had hit for such an average since the great Joe Dimaggio in the 1940s. Rodriguez discovered that fame can be quite a pain, according to a report in the *Sporting News* in the spring of 1997. He said:

> At times I think back to how it used to be. At times I wish for it to be simpler. I feel inadequate to keep up with the demands for some of my time, pieces of me. I mean, I love it . . . but at times I resent it.

Even when your dreams become reality in one area, it does not mean they come true in all aspects of life. Your career may be a great success, but you may still learn that "the boy don't always get the girl." Even the rich and powerful, those who have achieved their wildest dreams, have to deal with themselves and the same emptiness, frustration, and fear that challenge us all.

I remember visiting a seminary in Marin County, California, in the late 1970s. The professor who showed me around told me that Marin County was one of the wealthiest counties in America per capita but also had one of the highest suicide rates in the country. Success in one area did not prevent shattered dreams in other areas of life.

In the real world shattered dreams come in all shapes and sizes. Some people experience shattered dreams when they don't achieve their goals. Others achieve their goals but experience shattered dreams when they find that success doesn't meet their deepest needs. Life is not like the movies where the director can choose the ending of the story. We have to live through our stories, with the endings beyond our control.

Jesus told a parable about shattered dreams. It was my father's favorite Bible story and is one of mine. We refer to it as the parable of the Prodigal Son from Luke 15. It's the story of a young man and a father whose dreams were shattered.

The youngest son went to his father and demanded his inheritance immediately. He had his dreams and wanted the resources to start making them a reality right away. The father gave him his inheritance, and the boy went off in search of his dreams.

The boy spent his newfound wealth on wild living. The implication is that he blew it on booze and women. Soon he was broke. His dreams, whatever they were, did not materialize. He searched for his dream only to find it wasn't what he wanted. He was so broke that he did what no good Jewish boy would do: he got a job slopping the pigs.

The Bible says the boy came to his senses and told himself that even his father's hired hands had food to spare. He decided he would go home to Dad and tell him he had sinned against heaven and his father and ask to be hired as a common laborer.

His father saw him coming and ran down the road, threw his arms around him, and kissed him, proclaiming for all the world to hear that his son who was lost had been found. He then ordered that he be given a fine robe, sandals, and the family ring. Then they had a party to celebrate.

This parable contains profound truths. The boy's dreams of independence and success were shattered. He obviously dreamed of succeeding on his own, away from his father's shadow. He was a miserable failure. What he wanted the most did not bring him happiness. His dreams ended in a pig pen.

The story shows that the boy had a wrong understanding of success. He was dreaming the wrong kind of dreams. He did not realize until he "came to his senses" that he had it good at home. He was already loved and accepted and was considered a person of worth and value by his father and by God.

His father reinforced this when he got home by throwing a party and welcoming the boy back. The father in the story plays the role of God. God always loves us, rejoices in us, and loves us even in failure. The father reminds us that we can always come home. There is nothing we can do that is so bad we cannot return to God.

Yes, dreams are more likely not to come true than to be fulfilled. Still, it is important to dream, to strive, to reach for the stars. I would hate to think of living without having dreams and goals. Dreams add excitement to my life. If all you find is stardust, it doesn't mean the journey was not worthwhile, especially if it helped you come to your senses and know yourself. Every shattered dream is an opportunity to grow and learn as a disciple.

Another way to make the best of shattered dreams is to look realistically at what happened. Attaining a berth in the Final Four in NCAA basketball is a tremendous success, even if you do not win the national championship. Being a good pastor in any size church is a tremendous accomplishment. Having a marriage that survived 20 years and is still growing is a phenomenal achievement. Maybe every dream did not come true, but what did happen may be tremendous in and of itself.

One key to dealing with shattered dreams is to be wise enough not to take failure personally. Having a dream crash and burn does not make you a bad person. Your worth comes from God. It is not earned; it is a gift. This is the lesson the Prodigal Son learned and the lesson Chase had to learn. A shattered dream does not mean life is not worth living or that we are not persons of worth and value. It does not mean we have not accomplished, or at least learned, a great deal that will be very beneficial in the future.

Whether or not your dreams come true, what matters is the kind of person doing the dreaming. Emotionally healthy people are secure in their worth and handle failure and success equally well.

Life "often just turns out that way," but failure can't shatter your dreams when you are centered on who you are, not your success or failure. Everyone has regrets. The challenge is to be the same person whatever life does to your dreams and to adjust them to the reality of the moment. It's important not only to "come to your senses" when you've lost them, but also to do the work necessary to "keep your senses." Keep your feet on the ground while your head is in the clouds.

Living as a servant of God and using your gifts to meet the needs of others means the Glory Train stops by your door nearly every day. When your dreams are God's dreams, to be *who* God created you to be and do *what* God created you to do, handling incredible success and unbelievable failure takes on a whole new meaning. Whatever life brings, there will always be something left to do as long as you are alive. There will be another day to live, love, meet a need, or achieve a goal.

My mother is a tremendous inspiration to me. She is an 82-year-old live-wire. She is the volunteer librarian in the small town where she lives. She drives 30 miles to San Angelo to sing in a senior citizens church choir every Friday. She works one day a month in an antique store in another town. She plays the piano at church every Sunday. She travels all over the country to Baptist meetings. In her spare time she attends plays and drives people to the doctor. I wish I had her energy!

But from February 1980 until June 1989, Mother hardly left the house except for church services. My Dad had emphysema and spent the last five years of his life on oxygen. When he wanted something while in bed, he rang a little bell, and

Mother would go running to see what he wanted. He could be a little testy when she did not respond as fast as he wanted.

Watching my mother's exhausting, yet full, life these last 10 years since Dad died, I realize just how much she sacrificed taking care of him. But she never complained. She accepted the responsibilities that go along with loving someone without complaining. I still marvel at that love.

Certainly one of my mother's dreams was to be a good and faithful wife. She put many of her dreams and needs on hold while she stayed close to home. In truth, I guess she changed her dreams for those nine years. She made caring for my dad her dream. Maybe she let her dreams conform to reality. I think she dreamed the right kind of dreams, the dream of fulfilling her responsibilities. My mother could put her dreams and lifestyle on hold in order to live a different dream: caring for the man she would spend 54 years with. She could do this because life for her took place "in the real world."

Life often deals us a tough hand. Chase certainly was given a tough hand to play at an early age. Still, he and others like him need to keep dreaming. We all do. There will be many regrets, many failures. We will often venture into the desert of shattered dreams and end up with only regret, wondering if life will ever be good again.

The fact is, most of the time we dreamers will end up with regret and have to remind ourselves that we live "in the real world." As we experience success and failure, it is important to remember our source of worth—God—and our purpose for being—growth as a person and a life of service. Keeping these goals in front of us will help us deal with the desert of shattered dreams. As we survive this desert, we may realize that we have more to be thankful for than we have to regret.

Chapter 5

The Desert of Materialism

Harold was a big man, big in size and influence. He owned the largest timber company in East Texas. He was the largest contributor to First Baptist Church. He lived in the largest house in the county. Everybody knew Harold, and nearly everybody who knew him liked him. He had a huge personality and a big voice. His voice entered the room before his hulking frame. Harold had a tiny, petite wife. She was as popular as Harold and just as outgoing. Most people joked that Harold and Penny both talked so much that neither of them ever heard each other.

Harold's father had built the timber company. He had left the family farm in the 1920s, started the business from scratch, and built a family name as respected as his business. Harold took over in 1963. The business grew and grew. Then things changed.

The timber industry was dying in East Texas, had been for about 10 years. Harold never mentioned it to Penny, or if he did, she was talking at the same time and didn't hear him. For years he had been able to borrow money in Dallas to keep the business going. It also kept the hometown bankers from knowing his real situation. No one in town suspected any of Harold's problems. He continued to be the big man in the big house who was the big shot in the county.

Most people didn't believe it when they heard the news. They thought there must be some mistake. Not Harold, he would never do anything wrong. Just last year he had personally paid for the organ for the new worship center. He had also been the largest contributor to the building program, something he didn't talk about, but made sure others did.

It couldn't be true, but there it was in black and white. Harold was on the front page of the newspaper, head down, hands cuffed behind him. Harold had been arrested.

Over the next few weeks the details leaked out. Harold, who had been going broke for years, ignored financial reality as he maintained his lifestyle. He and several men from Dallas were charged with real estate fraud. Harold was convicted of fraud and sentenced to 10 years in prison. He declared bankruptcy. His house was sold to pay legal bills. The big shot everybody loved had become a destitute crook most people pitied.

Harold's story reminds me of Jesus' words in Matthew 6:19-21. We don't pay much attention to them, even in the community of believers called the church. We like our earthly treasures.

Do not store up for yourselves treasures on earth, where moth and rust destroy, and where thieves break in and steal. But store up for yourselves treasures in heaven, where moth and rust do not destroy, and where thieves do not break in and steal. For where your treasure is, there your heart will be also. (NIV)

I love the United States. I love the freedom of risk that goes with our system of government and our capitalist economic system. The United States is the richest country in the world. There are more Christians here per capita than in any other country. There are churches on every corner. Yet, in many ways, this is a sick society, both in personal and community ethics. We have a dark side, much of which is brought on by our personal and corporate greed.

The richest country in the world has a huge homeless population. Millions of children live in poverty and in single-parent homes. The United States has one of the highest child mortality rates in the developed world. Despite our riches, churches, and freedoms, we have one of the highest suicide rates in the world. Something is not right in this picture.

Conservative Christians, of which I am one, believe the Bible is a special book. It is to be our final authority in all matters of faith and practice. It is inspired, dependable, and truthful. We even fight among ourselves about how the Bible was inspired and how literally we should interpret it. We fight about the Bible sometimes more than we pay attention to it.

Many conservative Christians believe they must also be conservative politically, so there are groups such as the Christian Coalition and the Moral Majority. Politically conservative Christians tend to emphasize personal ethics. They are concerned about abortion, alcohol, pornography, and homosexuality. They acknowledge problems such as race relations, poverty, injustice, and environmental concerns, but these issues do not capture their heart and spirit. The real sign of faith for these politically active Christians is personal morality. However, that is not the perspective of Jesus or the Bible.

Jesus never mentioned homosexuality, abortion, or pornography. I am not saying these issues aren't serious moral issues in modern society. The corporate church and individual Christians need to address these issues, albeit with grace and respect for differing interpretations of Scripture.

Jesus addressed some very important issues, including the danger of possessions and the importance of helping the poor. In fact, Jesus talked about these issues more than any other subject. In Matthew and Mark one of every ten verses deals with these issues. In Luke it is one of every seven verses. Why did Jesus talk about this issue so much? Probably because "where your treasure is, there your heart will be also."

Willie Nelson sings a classic song about possessions titled "Heartaches of a Fool." The song describes the "fools for the dollar," who don't realize that "happiness and love are sent from heaven above." When I hear "Heartaches of a Fool," it prompts me to think about my ethical responsibilities in terms of my relationship with the land and with possessions.

I love the land. My family came to Paint Rock, Texas, in 1879. I am the fourth generation to raise sheep and cattle on the same land. I have told my sons that one freedom they do not have is to sell the family ranch. That piece of dirt has played a prominent role in my life, even my spiritual life.

In 1979 a close friend told me, "I would like to recommend you to be the chaplain [at a North Carolina Baptist university], but I know you won't do it. You have God limited to one geographical spot on the map." He was right. That night I wrote God a prayer where I admitted I did not want to serve Him in a place that kept me from being able to get to that "geographical spot on the map." I told God I really did want to serve Him, but that He knew how important family, heritage, and roots were to me and that I hoped He could work it out so I could fulfill my calling as a minister and still live close to home.

I am not saying I understand it all. All I know is that I have led a statewide Texas Baptist organization for 11 years. My sense of being where God wants me to be in His service could not be stronger. I live 26 miles from the house where I grew up and 38 miles from my ranch. When I need to take a day off to work cattle, I can do it. No questions asked. I am a fortunate man. God worked it out. I also know that ultimately I told God, "Wherever you lead, I'll go." And then He led me where I always wanted to be, at least geographically speaking.

In Hebrew thought, land was not simply dirt. It had a social and spiritual significance. Walter Brueggemann wrote that "land is never simply physical dirt but is always physical dirt freighted with social meaning derived from historical experience."

From the call of Abraham in which land was first promised to him and his posterity, to specific teachings in the Mosaic covenant about the Sabbath Year and the Year of Jubilee, to the writings of the prophets, there is a close connection between God's chosen people and the earth. The people of the Old Testament could not imagine one having a right relationship with God without having a right relationship with the land. The two were forever joined in their thought.

Justice was an important word in relation to the land. Land and the fruits of the land were to be distributed fairly. The land belonged to God. The role of humans was that of steward, a word that described a person who cared for the property of another. A person's stewardship was to result in justice for the land and society.

Harold in our case study got trapped in the desert of materialism. He got caught up in what was his—his property and his status. When he began to worship the god of things—of prestige and of power—he lost his perspective. He ignored his values. He ended up with the 'heartaches of a fool."

Jesus told a story in Luke 12 called the parable of the Rich Fool. It is the story of a rich farmer who produced a bumper crop. He thought to himself, "What shall I do? I have no place to store my crops." So he decided to tear down all his barns and build bigger ones. He told himself that he would have plenty stored away for years to come and that he could relax and eat, drink and be merry. God called him a fool. God told him he was going to die that night and asked him who was going to get all he had prepared for himself. Jesus concluded the story by saying, "This is how it will be with anyone who stores up things for himself but is not rich toward God."

Materialism is a dangerous desert, particularly in the United States where we have such riches. The desire for more and more can be insatiable. The temptation to define our worth by what we have, by our possessions, is reinforced by society. We equate success with wealth and possessions. Jesus did not use that standard.

"Heartaches of a Fool" prompts me to remember the proper relationship between people and possessions. The song reminds me of all the things that have been done in the name of God, which were really done selfishly and with little regard for the consequences. The song reminds me that the people in my life—my family and friends—are much more valuable than the things I own.

To avoid the desert of materialism, the Bible gives us some good principles. First, we really do not own anything. Everything belongs to God. That piece of dirt in West Texas may have had the Currie name on it since 1879, but it does not belong to me; it belongs to God. The concept of the tithe in the Old Testament, of giving away 10 percent of your income, is not a principle designed to finance church work and ministry. That is a secondary, although important, result. The meaning is much deeper. The concept of the tithe was instituted by God as a teaching tool. Giving money and possessions away reminds us that, in truth, we do not own anything. Someone who cannot share is living with the illusion that they own possessions when, actually, they are owned by their possessions.

Second, my role in relation to the land and all my possessions is that of a steward. I am to care for the possessions I control for the real owner—God. I cannot use the land or my money for my selfish desires. I am to use possessions I control in a way that furthers God's redemptive work.

Third, as a steward, I have no right to destroy that which is not mine. I do not have the right to pollute a river to improve my net income. I do not have the right to destroy a creature God created to pad my pocketbook. A Christian who is not an environmentalist should be a contradiction. For the Christian, God is the owner of possessions, and all are to be treated with respect and concern.

Fourth, profit cannot be the bottom line for a Christian. Certainly any business needs profit to survive, provide jobs, and prosper. Profit is good, but it is not good when it is extracted from the backs of underpaid workers and at the expense of the land, water, and air upon which we all depend.

I consider myself a Christian capitalist. I like the capitalist system and the freedom and incentive it provides. But my capitalism is tempered by my faith. I am a steward of what is not mine. Being a steward of possessions carries with it the responsibility to use those possessions in an ethical manner.

The United States is considered the most Christian nation in the world. It is also the country with the largest disparity between rich and poor in the industrialized world. This is just one example of how Christians have ignored the teachings of Scripture and bought into the value system of the world. The head of the Rockefeller Foundation said he considered this disparity to be one of the "most insidious and dangerous trends in this country. Why? Because countries with income extremes have a great difficulty functioning democratically."

It almost seems, reflecting on the lyrics in "Heartaches of a Fool," that we as Americans started out with the dreams and plans of someone wise but ended up with the heartaches of a fool. We have built our bigger barns but failed to realize that "happiness and love" are sent from above.

The desert of materialism is a constant temptation. To avoid this desert, we need the courage to stand up against everything society says is right and good. The most important source of courage is having a proper sense of self-worth. Our value comes from God, not from our possessions or our status in society.

Chapter 6

The Desert of Anger

I don't handle anger well, but I handle it better than I used to. At least I express it better, more responsibly, especially with my family. I seldom blow up. I get less angry about things, but it is still a problem for me.

One problem is that anger can be enjoyable. Holding a grudge can be one of life's most destructive pleasures. For example, I have so much respect for Tom Landry that I still enjoy watching Jerry Jones, the current owner of the Dallas Cowboys, who fired Tom Landry, in anguish when his team loses. I have a great deal of respect for Emmitt Smith, Troy Aikman, and many other Cowboys, but I enjoy rooting against the owner. That kind of anger is pretty innocent. I really do not mean Jerry Jones any harm. I just want him to sell the Cowboys so I can root for them again!

The song "Heart of the Matter," written by Don Henley, is nearly a hymn to me. The message it conveys about forgiveness sounds like Jesus' words to forgive "seventy times seven." It says to "put it all behind you" because if "you keep carryin' that anger, it'll eat you up inside."

We live in an age when people are angry and filled with rage. We seldom show grace to others. We fill our lives with pride and competition and then wonder why we have so few friends. If anyone crosses us or treats us wrong, we promise to pay them back, often starting an endless cycle of verbal or physical violence.

People say Bob used to be different. They talk about a man who was quick with a smile, always ready to lend a helping hand. His co-workers said he was especially good to have around during a crisis. He had a soothing manner about him that encouraged others to put their differences aside and work toward a common goal. He encouraged people to stay calm during a crisis and examine the situation before reacting. He was considered a valuable employee who was in charge of the entire trust department at the largest independently owned bank in his small town.

Nobody thought much about it when the bank sold. Banks were merging every day. The financial business was changing. The motto was, "Get big or get out." The first sale did not affect the bank employees very much. Bob's bank was purchased by another bank from Fort Worth. It had purchased several small-town banks.

When the bank sold again 18 months later, this time to a holding company with banks in 17 states, the employees became a little more concerned. They had reason to be. Within three months Bob was without a job.

People say that's when Bob started to change. It was easy to notice. Bob wrote a letter to the editor of the local newspaper at least once a month. It was always about the unfairness of the big corporations. Soon his letters began to attack the government, claiming they were behind all the mergers.

Bob enjoyed his anger. Soon he looked for other targets. He became a regular at school board, city council, and county commission meetings. He always had something to say. He fought any hint of a tax increase at all levels. He fought any new approach to providing government services. He fought zoning changes. He fought new technology in the school system. He even griped about the football coaches.

It became clear that Bob did not have his own opinion as much as he formed his opinion based on what others thought. If an "official body" held a position, Bob held the opposite view.

Bob's friends began to find excuses not to play golf or fish with him. If someone had a good idea, Bob had a better idea. If someone had a good fish story, Bob had a better one. If someone's kids had accomplished something, Bob's kids had accomplished even more.

Church was no different. For a long time no one could decide if Bob was for the new building or against it. If the discussion was leaning towards building a new sanctuary, Bob rose to speak against such an extravagant expenditure. Later, when the discussion was dominated by those opposed to building a new worship center, Bob rose to speak about how bad the current facilities were, proclaiming he had experienced a change of heart.

The problem was, since Bob had been fired, he never had a change of heart. He got angry about being fired, stayed mad about it, and found other things to dislike. Bob was an angry man who felt he had lost his position of influence in the community. Therefore, he spent the rest of his life proclaiming to everyone who would listen how important he still was. He had an opinion on everything, so he must be important, he thought.

The desert of anger can be deceptively appealing. All of us have known people who have lied to us, broken promises to us, let us down, and hurt our pride. None of these experiences is pleasant. It is only normal to feel hurt. When we feel hurt, we feel threatened. The natural response to feeling threatened is to feel anger. Anger is natural. It is neither moral nor immoral. The problem with anger is how it is expressed and handled.

The best presentation I have ever heard on anger was given by David and Vera Mace, who had been marriage counselors for more than 50 years when I heard them speak. They announced to the audience that they had recently discovered that most of their life's work had not been dealing with the real problem in relationships. Marriage problems boiled down to a problem of how to deal with anger in any given situation.

The Maces' presentation centered around the breakdown of a marriage relationship but had meaning for anger in general, including that held by Bob in our story. The Maces shared the following points: (1) When a marriage ends in divorce or a family breaks down, the failure takes place from the inside. (2) The supposed causes of marital trouble—difficulties with sex, money, in-laws, and childrearing—are not the real causes. These are only the arenas in which the inner failure of the relationship is outwardly demonstrated. (3) The inner failure of a close relationship always takes place for the same reason—because the persons involved have been unable to achieve mutual love and intimacy. (4) The failure to achieve love and intimacy is almost always due to the inability of the persons concerned to deal creatively with anger.

According to the Maces, people generally handle anger in one of two ways: either they vent it or deny it. Both of these methods are destructive to love and intimacy. There is a third way to handle anger, and this method allows anger to be used constructively. It involves acknowledging the anger, not feeling guilty about it, and not acting on it inappropriately. Then, at an appropriate time, when emotion has subsided, work through why you felt angry in the first place. That is, why did you feel threatened? If another person has a been a part of your anger, especially your spouse, then discuss your anger and feelings with that person. In this way anger becomes a means of building intimacy rather than destroying it.

Bob had every right to feel angry. He had lost his job, one he had been good at and found gratifying. Life dealt him a cruel blow, and being angry about it was perfectly normal. Bob just never worked through the anger to allow the experience to be beneficial to him. He related to everyone out of his anger and lost his friends and his influence in his church and community.

There is a good example in the Scriptures of the proper role of anger. Paul was angry when he wrote the book of Galatians. It is a letter to the churches in Galatia, not just one church, but all of them. It appears that there were those in the churches called "Judaizers." A Judaizer was a Jewish Christian who believed that a Gentile (non-Jew) had to become a Jew before he could become a Christian. In order to become a Jew, a Gentile had to be circumcised. Paul considered this an effort to "pervert the gospel of grace." It was a step back into the old legalism, the effort to earn a relationship with God rather than accept the love of God as a free gift. It negated the importance of the death of Christ.

Paul pulled no punches in expressing his anger. He wrote in Galatians 1: "As we have already said, so now I say again, if anybody is preaching to you a gospel other than what you accepted, let him be eternally condemned." This is strong language. Paul went on to give his credentials. He wrote that he was a good Jew, advancing in Judaism quickly, far beyond what most people his age were accomplishing, and he was "extremely zealous for the traditions of the fathers."

Peter had fallen in with the Judaizers, so Paul said he "opposed Peter to his face" for his hypocrisy. Finally, Paul concluded by reminding them that "the only thing that counts is faith expressing itself through love." Evidently, Paul also felt that standing up to those he viewed as perverting the gospel was an act of love. In Galatians 5:12 Paul was so angry, he wrote: "As for those agitators, I wish they would go all the way and emasculate themselves!" Ouch!

What do the Maces, Paul, and the song "Heart of the Matter" say to us about dealing with the desert of anger? First, they show us that anger is normal. Paul had a right to be angry. The beliefs he was willing to die for were being threatened. In "Heart of the Matter" the singer is also angry with good reason; his heart has been broken.

Second, these examples show us how to use anger. The Maces teach us to use anger constructively, to learn about ourselves from our anger, and to examine our insecurities and weaknesses. Paul shows us the importance of expressing our anger when others misrepresent the truth. Certainly it is important to be angry at lying, racism, and duplicity by ourselves and others. It is important not to sweep things under the rug. Some things are important enough to work up a good "mad" and try to do something about, but in a constructive manner.

Dr. Martin Luther King, Jr. was one of my heroes. He was a courageous example of righteous anger, of someone angry in love, trying to right wrongs while still loving the oppressor. He got the angriest at those who stood on the sidelines during the civil rights movement. He confronted them in love, but forcefully. Recorded in his book, *I Have a Dream*, are these words he spoke at the funeral of four young girls killed during Sunday School in the bombing of a Birmingham church:

> Yet they died nobly. They are the martyred heroines of a holy crusade for freedom and human dignity. So they have something to say to us in their death. They have something to say to every minister of the gospel who has remained silent behind the safe security of stained-glass windows. They have something to say to every politician who has fed his constituents the stale bread of hatred and the soiled

meat of racism. . . . They have something to say to every
Negro who passively accepts the evil system of segregation
and stands on the sidelines in the midst of a mighty struggle for justice. They say to each of us, black and white alike,
that we must substitute courage for caution.[1]

What a positive, creative, redemptive use of anger. King used
his anger and disappointment to challenge us all to become a
part of the solution instead of a part of the problem.

Anger can also teach us about ourselves. The Maces say we
get angry when we are afraid or threatened. Examining situations in which we responded in anger can enlighten us about
our insecurities and fears. Dealing with what makes us feel
afraid and threatened can lead to the avoidance of anger. We
may discover that many of our fears are totally unwarranted
and thus reduce the situations in our lives where we respond
with anger.

Jealously is a simple illustration. Often we have no reason
to feel jealous of a spouse or a work colleague if we examine
the situation more closely. The situation may not be threaten-
ing except in our heads.

Don Henley's song describes the most valuable tool we can
use to deal with anger—forgiveness. Forgiveness is powerful. It
has the power to free us for the future. The healthiest way to
deal with disappointment and mistreatment is to forgive the
wrongdoer.

Forgiveness does not mean we have to continue a relationship with the wrongdoer. It does not mean we have to decide
that the actions of the wrongdoer were actually moral and correct. It does not mean we do not confront the wrongdoer
about the deed. Forgiveness does mean to confront in a
redemptive manner and without bitterness.

Living out of forgiveness means taking specific actions.
Often, out of our anger, we punish people who do not please
us. We are especially prone to do this with our spouses and
children. This expression of anger is very unproductive.

Forgiveness means we do not punish others just because they live differently from us.

Roy Austin, a Dallas counselor, helped me see the difference between making a demand and making a request. He said that we should make very few demands in a relationship. It is much better to make requests of people and leave them free to make their own decision about responding to the request.

We should never punish someone with words or actions just because they choose not to honor our requests. Since we want people to love us and interpret it as an act of love for them to try and please us, we often get angry and seek to punish those who do not please us. This destroys the relationship. It is much better to make a request, and if the request is not honored, respond in forgiveness. This will work wonders to ease anger.

Sometimes we have to practice self-forgiveness because the person we are angriest with is ourself. Like the apostle Paul in Romans 7, we know what is right but do the wrong thing anyway. Then we spend an enormous amount of energy trying to "justify our bloody deeds." Rationalization and deception are not good responses to our own moral failures. We cannot lie to ourselves about our actions and learn from them. The fact is, we are selfish, self-centered people. That is why we need Jesus. The gospel is for the weak, the fallen, the losers—that is, all of us. Even as we grow in our relationship with God, the old nature is constantly at battle with the new one inside us. The old nature wins much more than we like to admit. When that happens, the one door to growth is through forgiveness.

We must accept God's forgiveness and forgive ourselves. Forgiveness means we set the wrongdoer free. Freedom means we set ourselves free. We do not carry the experience with us. If we do, the anger eats us up on the inside, just as Henley wrote in the song.

When Jesus sent his disciples from town to town, he told them they would be rejected in some cities. He encouraged them to shake the dust from their feet and go to the next place. It was important not to carry the experience and the anger it generated with them to the next place. The bitterness would affect their work in the next location. John Claypool says this is an analogy of "leaving the experience behind them."

To forgive is one of the most powerful decisions a person can make. Forgiveness allows us to go on with our lives and experience new love and adventure. Forgiveness allows others to grow and learn from their experiences. Forgiveness opens the possibility for healing in the most broken of relationships. Anger, held on to and cherished, prevents any of these possibilities from becoming a reality.

The best way to deal with our anger is to acknowledge it, handle it responsibly, learn from it, forgive others if they contributed to it, and move on to what new thing God may be doing in our lives.

Notes

[1]Martin Luther King, Jr., *I Have a Dream: Writings That Changed the World* (San Francisco: Harper, 1986) 116.

Chapter 7

The Desert of Playing the Victim

Marilyn had not been happily married. Everyone who knew her was aware of that. She and Stan lived separately together. They each had their own friends. They often took vacations apart. Stan liked to take his vacation time hunting in Colorado, while Marilyn preferred a week at the beach.

No one close to them was surprised when Stan had an affair. Most people wondered who would have an affair first. When Stan moved out and filed for divorce, their friends thought it opened up the possibility of growth for both of them, and maybe even future happiness if they used the divorce as a catalyst to examine their lives and work on personal issues.

Marilyn didn't see it that way. Yes, the divorce helped her to have meaning and purpose in her life, if you can call hating someone a reason to live. But she did not expend any discipline looking at her own issues. Marilyn became consumed with hating Stan, talking about Stan, despising Stan. You could not have a conversation with Marilyn without hearing what a slime-ball Stan was, what a horrible father he was, how he took financial advantage of his elderly parents, and what a worthless person he was. She loved to tell how badly he had taken advantage of her. He had left her with no money. He was always late with child support. He did not take the kids at Christmas and other holidays.

The truth was, Marilyn did everything possible to keep Stan from seeing the kids, and she pestered him constantly for money to buy things over and above the child support he paid faithfully. Stan had been more than generous in the divorce settlement.

Marilyn loved being the victim. It defined her life and gave her a reason to get up in the morning. She played the victim with anyone who would listen to her. If you tried to point these truths out to her, she cut you off. You just didn't understand her life, how tough it was. Her job was horrible. She was underpaid, no matter how much of a raise she received. Her co-workers constantly took advantage of her. Life was the pits, and none of it was Marilyn's responsibility.

Marilyn never dated another man longer than a month. Her dates quickly realized that the only conversation Marilyn could have was about how bad Stan had taken advantage of her. To know Marilyn was to think of Linda Rondstat singing "Poor, Poor, Pitiful Me."

The children grew up with no concept of responsibility. All Marilyn had ever shown them was how to blame their dad for any problem she might have, whether it be financial, emotional, or personal. The kids grew up blaming their teachers for their poor grades, their coaches for their bad attitude in athletics, and their dad for everything else. Of course, Marilyn consistently supported their viewpoint.

Years passed, and Marilyn never changed. She never got over it. She never even tried. Anger ate her up on the inside. Without her anger Marilyn had no identity. She was the victim, but as miserable as she was, she loved every minute of it.

It is easy to walk in the desert of playing the victim. All you have to do is refuse to take responsibility for your life. Blame it on someone else, on circumstances beyond your control. Blame it on heredity, your boss, your race, your kids, your ex. Ultimately, if you work at it hard enough, you can blame your failures and emptiness on God.

Two songs stand out to me as songs written from the perspective of a victim. I really like both songs because, in truth, I enjoy allowing myself to feel like a victim. When I first heard "Untanglin' My Mind," written by Clint Black and Merle Haggard, I jokingly told my wife to make sure it was played at my funeral so that everyone would know I died because "you finally drove me crazy, and I've gone to untangle my mind." She laughed because one of the joys of our marriage is that we are able to kid each other and laugh a great deal.

Another song that allows to me to go back in time and feel like a victim is "Reno," co-written by Doug Supernaw. "Reno" reminds me of several specific long-ago romances in which I felt the person "didn't have a heart" and didn't care when I was down. I felt used and abused and victimized. I felt I had opened myself up to another person as honestly as I could and had been rejected. It hurt, and I hung on to the pain for a long time. "Reno" reminds me that I've enjoyed playing the victim in the past.

I personally don't feel much sympathy for persons who play the victim, although I've done my share of it from time to time. Disappointment is a normal part of life. Everyone has been hurt. Most of us move on. All of us can move on, if we choose.

It is interesting that the person in the desert of isolation is easier to feel sorry for than the person trapped in the desert of playing the victim. Both have been hurt. Both have made unhealthy choices. It may be that we are more sympathetic to those in isolation because they keep the pain to themselves. Persons playing the victim act out their role publicly and loudly. They thrust their pain in our faces all the time. They are constantly reminding us that "they couldn't roll a seven" if you gave them loaded dice. Bad things always happen to them, and if good things happen, they don't notice. They view all of life from the perspective of a victim.

Some of our harshness is justified. Bad things do happen to all of us, but most people do not milk the experience for all it's worth. We have sympathy for people going through a tough experience. We care. We want to help—for awhile. But we also don't have much patience. In time, we expect people to get over it. When they don't, we move away from them. We move on with our lives, despite the pain, and we expect others to do the same.

Jesus had an encounter with a man who was playing the victim. There was a pool near the Sheep Gate in Jerusalem called Bethesda. Apparently, an angel would stir the water, and whoever got in first would be healed. Therefore, a great number of disabled people—the blind, the lame, the paralyzed—would lie around the pool waiting for the water to be stirred.

One man had been there for 38 years. When Jesus heard about the man and how long he had been there, he asked the man an interesting question: "Do you want to get well?" Instead of answering the question, the man gave his excuse. He said that he had no one to help him get into the pool, so someone else always got in ahead of him. Jesus healed the man and told him to "get up and walk." Later he told him to live right or something worse would happen to him.

The man was playing the victim. He did not really want to get well, and Jesus recognized this. He had become so identified with his problem that it defined his being. He had become the one person who couldn't be healed—"poor, poor, pitiful me." He liked to go out by the pool and rake in all the sympathy he could get.

The fact is, surviving the desert of playing the victim is no different than surviving any other desert. It requires paradoxical truth—compassion and confrontation.

Jesus was compassionate with people going through life's trials and tribulations. He showed compassion in his dealings with other people, especially the outcasts of Jewish society such as the Samaritan woman. He showed compassion by even talking to her. That very act broke many Jewish laws because Jews and Samaritans did not associate with each other. Samaritans were considered racial and religious half-breeds. They were the result of intermarriage between Jews and Gentiles. Furthermore, in that society men did not talk with women. Jesus had a conversation with the Samaritan woman as if she were his equal in society. Many of Jesus' teachings were very radical in regard to money, social issues, and religious law. His actions were even more radical.

The Samaritan woman had lived a hard life. Jesus was tender with her. He told her about the "living water" he had and offered it to her. In the process Jesus confronted her as he let the woman know that accepting this water meant facing the real truth about herself.

She commented that she had no husband, which Jesus said he knew, but he also informed her that she had had five husbands and the man she was living with wasn't her husband. Talk about a reality check! But Jesus spoke with compassion. He let the woman know that playing games would not be a part of their conversation.

No one will stop playing the victim until they are ready to face the real world, the truth about their circumstances, and take responsibility for the part they played in creating their current situation. Victims need compassion, but they also need "tough love," because many victims get stuck playing the part. As the lyrics say, they operate from the perspective that "there ain't no way to win." They need people who will not be enablers in their lives, people who will not support their playing the victim.

The result of playing the victim is that we can't get what we really want: a new chance at love and life. We have to risk losing what has become comfortable, what has become our identity. We have to give up playing the victim.

Ultimately, persons playing the victim have to decide if they really want to get well. If they say yes, then they need the love and support of counselors and others who will walk the delicate line between compassion and confrontation. Even with the help of Jesus it is very difficult to pick up your mat and walk out of the desert of playing the victim because you have decided to get over it. Getting over it will be long process. It will take much work and discipline. It will be painful. The process does begin, though, when you decide you want to get well and "untangle your mind." Being a victim is the easy part; getting over it is a much tougher role.

Chapter 8

The Desert of Pride

My dad's idea of a vacation contained only two possibilities: going to a baseball game or going to the mountains of New Mexico or Colorado. Both destinations were fine with me. In 1996 I took my sons to the Baseball Hall of Fame and to watch the Yankees, Red Sox, Mets, and Phillies. It was a wonderful father-son experience that my own father and I had in 1976. I also love the mountains. Just like with my dad, I continue to stop at the historical sites in New Mexico to show my sons Billy the Kid's grave and to go through the old museums.

The earliest memory I have of a television show is "Billy the Kid," starring Clu Glulager. I guess I got hooked on outlaws from watching "Billy the Kid" in the 1950s and going on vacations out West. I like to read about outlaws and can watch *Butch Cassidy and the Sundance Kid* at least once a year. One of the members of the "Hole in the Wall" gang of Butch and Sundance was Harvey Logan, alias Kid Curry. That was my college nickname. Another gang member was from the county where I grew up. In one Old West book I found a copy of a poster wanting him for killing a man in Painted Rock, Texas, my hometown.

Lots of songs are about outlaws, but my favorite is "Desperado" by the Eagles. The entire album seems to be about the Dalton Gang. While I am sure the Eagles had no intention of conveying a religious message in the songs, I hear a great deal about pride in the lyrics.

Every Old West book about outlaws has a section on the Dalton Gang. The story of the Daltons is interesting. They were distant cousins of Frank and Jesse James. Their mother was an aunt of the Younger brothers who were in the James gang, although their careers did not run parallel.

Early in their history the Daltons were a law-abiding family. Frank Dalton, the oldest son, was a deputy U.S. marshal who was killed in the line of duty in 1887. Bill Dalton was an attorney in California and some say a member of the California State Assembly. Grat, Bob, and Emmett Dalton also became U.S. deputy marshals after Frank's death. They were respected lawmen until something happened. The stories differ. Some say Bob was fired for taking bribes. Others say he quit because of the corruption he found. Soon Grat and Emmett were fired over rumors of cattle rustling. The Daltons turned to crime about 1890, eight years after Jesse James was killed.

They crossed over to the other side of the law, with middle brother Bob the leader of the gang. In and around Kansas, Missouri, and the Indian Territories, they robbed banks, trains, and gambling games. Finally, plans were made for one last daring bank robbery. Bob wanted to do something even his cousins, the James Gang, had never done. The Dalton Gang would rob two banks at once in broad daylight.

Disguised with fake mustaches and beards, Bob, Grat, Emmett, and two other men rode into their hometown of Coffeyville, Kansas, on October 5, 1892. Bob and Emmett successfully robbed the First National Bank, but Grat and the other two men had trouble at the Condon Bank. The banker successfully stalled them several minutes, pretending the safe was on a time lock and wouldn't be open for a couple of minutes.

Those few minutes allowed the citizens, who had recognized the gang, time to get their weapons. As the bandits left the banks, the streets filled with bullets. The gang ran up the alley for their horses, guns blazing. All were shot numerous times. Only Emmett survived, even though he was shot several times.

Emmett, only 20 at the time, went on to serve more than 14 years in prison, but he lived an honorable life after that. He helped with a silent movie about the Coffeyville raid in 1909 and then worked as a consultant in the movie industry. He also made public service features about the evils of crime that were shown in the movie theaters. He died in 1937.

Bill Doolin was not with the Dalton Gang when they attempted this daring robbery. Why? The answer lies in what you choose to believe. Eyewitnesses say there were six riders while the gang was still a few miles out of town. The other rider was supposedly Bill Doolin. Some say that Doolin's horse became lame so he turned back to steal another and was too late to participate in the hold-up. Others say he faked his horse being lame because he had a bad feeling about the plan and turned back.

After the Daltons were killed, Bill Doolin formed the Doolin Gang with several other former members of the Dalton Gang. Presumably, Doolin planned to quit the outlaw life in 1896 and move to New Mexico or West Texas after falling in love and marrying a minister's daughter. He picked up his wife at her parents' house late one night and was riding beside her in a buggy when he was shot in an ambush by waiting lawmen.

The really interesting story is Bill Dalton. Remember the lyrics from the "Doolin-Dalton Reprise"?

> Go down Bill Dalton, it must be God's will,
> Two brothers lyin' dead in Coffeyville.
> Two voices call to you from where they stood,
> Lay down your law books . . .

Bill Dalton returned to Kansas after his two brothers had been killed as outlaws and while another was in prison. He became an outlaw and teamed up with Bill Doolin. Doolin was clearly the leader of the gang. This is as close as it gets to a historical Doolin-Dalton gang. Bill Dalton did not survive long as an outlaw. Bill Dalton was shot in 1895 after lawmen found him at his home.

These men are what I call "desperados." They're the kind of legendary characters the Eagles sang about in their album, *Desperado*. The songs seem to tie together into one story about Bill Dalton. To me, pride is a key ingredient in the story. I can hear pride in "Doolin-Dalton," "Twenty-One," "Outlaw Man," "Certain Kind of Fool," and "Desperado."

Bob Dalton's pride made him want to be as famous as his cousin, Jesse James. In fact, he wanted to outdo Jesse. Bill Dalton's pride led him back to Kansas to follow in the footsteps of his brothers and avenge their deaths. The desert of pride can be dangerous. It is dangerous when we allow our pride to push us to try to be a "big shot," to be more than we were created to be.

Outlaws are not the only ones to live in the desert of pride. The Pharisees in Jesus' era lived there, too. They were the religious authorities, the experts on the Law. They knew all the rules and made sure everyone knew that they knew. They were so sure they knew everything there was to know about

God that when God acted, they could not see His work in Jesus. They knew so much, they couldn't believe. They lacked faith; they relied on knowledge.

The Pharisees spent much of their time and energy trying to trap Jesus and destroy him because he was a threat to their authority. They claimed they represented God, so they told people how to worship God. Jesus, with his emphasis on grace, meeting needs whether it was technically the right day to do so or not, messed up their system and threatened their standing in the community. Jesus described them as men of pride who did not really love God. He said they did everything for others to see, not for God. Their worth came from the opinions of others.

A specific illustration makes Jesus' point. In the story of the Pharisee and the tax collector, the Pharisee stood up and prayed, "God, I thank you I am not like all the other men—robbers, evildoers, adulterers—or even like this tax collector." The tax collector simply said, "God, have mercy on me, a sinner." Jesus said the tax collector went home justified, "for everyone who exalts himself will be humbled, and he who humbles himself will be exalted." The Pharisee's prayer is the perfect illustration of someone stranded in the desert of pride. Pharisees based their worth and salvation on themselves rather than on God.

C. S. Lewis called pride the "great sin." He wrote in *Mere Christianity* that pride is the essential vice, the utmost evil. "Pride leads to every other vice: it is the complete anti-God state of mind." According to Lewis, the real problem with pride is that a proud person cannot know God. Since God is always superior to us, we cannot see God while we are busy looking down on others.

Lewis described pride as essentially competitive in nature. A proud person is not proud at being rich or beautiful or clever but at being richer or more beautiful or clever than others. Pride enjoys power. The Pharisees and the Dalton

Gang craved power. The songs on the *Desperado* album describe a man thirsty for power, recognition, and immortality.

One problem with pride is denial, the inability to perceive the reality of who we really are. Someone who is trapped in the desert of pride is out of touch with their own weaknesses and incapable of learning. Remember, the key characteristic of a disciple is teachability, not morality. Why did Jesus call disciples who were tax collectors, fishermen, and others from the lower end of the class system? They were teachable. They knew their weaknesses, their sinfulness, and their needs. That is why the "poor in spirit," those who are aware of their own brokenness, will see God.

Someone once described sin as either trying to be more than you were created to be or settling to be less. People in the desert of pride have forgotten they are creatures, not the Creator. They strive for power, control, influence, and status. They are self-absorbed. They want to be God. They reject their status as a child of God and seek to become God. They seek to be more than human.

Pride is centered in selfishness. Pride is reveling in who we are and what we have accomplished, not in God. Unhealthy pride stems from an improper self-image, the idea that we are self-made people. Pride also costs us in terms of relationships.

It saddens me to think of people living without meaningful relationships. They are "spending their time with their pride." I think of parents estranged from their children because their pride will not let them forgive, people who are unable to say, "I'm sorry." I picture people who are feeling separated from God because their pride will not allow them to admit their desperate need for love and meaning in their sad, empty lives. They spend their time with their pride rather than with God and others who would love them if they would only be open to the wonderful experience.

Having written about the evils of pride, let me say a positive word about it. There are two kinds of pride. One kind is healthy; one is not. Healthy pride comes from self-respect, self-appreciation, and self-acceptance. Healthy pride encourages us to use our talents, to strive to be the best and never quit. Healthy pride is not our attempt to earn our worth, but our attempt to live up to our gifts and commitments.

Pride is good when its source is properly understood. True healthy pride comes from God. The source of our pride should be God and the fact that we are loved by God and created in the image of God. That means there are no unimportant people. All persons have value based on God's system, not the world's or society's. We do not earn our worth; it comes as a gift. The secret, then, is to live out of that gift.

The key is to have a proper self-image. People are not important because of their talent, their physical beauty, their money, or their success. Society judges on that basis. Our worth comes from God. We are important because God says so, not because of anyone else or what we accomplish.

People with a proper self-image are able to be servants. Many people will do good things that get their names in the newspaper and give them recognition at church or in the community. The truly healthy individual is able to serve, to be a part of ministering to people whether or not anyone knows. The world is truly helped with servants, not publicity-seekers.

People without healthy pride forget they are creations of God. They settle for nothingness. They have no goals, no dreams, no desire to serve. They turn to sex, drugs, crime, work, whatever, seeing life in the smallest, most basic of terms. They reject their status as children of God, living out of the flesh totally, rejecting their spiritual capabilities. They settle for being *only* flesh like any other creature. They deny their spiritual dimension.

The lyrics to "Saturday Night," from *Desperado*, bring up a sentimental emotion in me that relates to healthy pride, especially the lyrics about the railroad and the boards on the windows.

My dad loved railroads. One of my favorite memories is his taking my sister and me to get on the train at midnight to ride to Dallas where Mother was visiting her sister. Dad had told me he was going with us but told me to not tell my sister because he wanted to surprise her. It was our first train ride, or at least the first one I remember. It is a special memory.

I like old things, family things. My wife and I sleep in a four-poster bed that belonged to my Uncle Bill. Our dining room table was my Grandmother Currie's. Our piano belonged to Aunt Mary. The workbenches in my shop were my Grandfather Patton's, then my Dad's, and now mine. I hunt quail with Uncle Willard's Browning 12-gauge. I hunt deer with my Dad's 300-savage, which is at least 75 years old.

I believe it is healthy for individuals to own their roots and take pride in who they are and where they've come from. Many people get trapped in the desert of pride trying to prove they are better than their family, their small-town upbringing, or their economic background.

Pride is a fascinating concept. It can help you stand up for what is right, or it can help you destroy yourself trying to earn what you already have—complete worth and value. Pride can give you the courage to go the extra mile, to dig deep into your soul and prevail, or it can keep you from all meaningful relationships. No meaningful relationship can survive without humility and forgiveness, even your relationship with yourself.

Pride is an interesting paradox. Each one of us is wonderfully important to be so terribly insignificant. We can take pride in who we are in Christ, remembering how insignificant we are in the eyes of the world. More importantly, we know we do not have to prove anything to the world, for the world has no worth or credit or status to give us that can touch what we have already been given. God made us. Christ died for us. We are very important. Share the good news. Living in the desert of pride will never earn for you something better than what you have already been given—the unconditional love and acceptance of God.

Chapter 9

The Desert of Emptiness

The desert of emptiness seems to be the desert most mentioned in songs. This is probably because good writing comes out of our own experiences, and all of us have experienced loneliness and emptiness. Many songs reflect the human desire to find meaning and purpose in life, or at the very least, a little comfort amidst the pain. The haunting lyrics from the Eagles' "Doolin-Dalton Reprise" speak to me of the things we try in our human attempts to fill the painful emptiness of our existence—"easy money and faithless women, you will never kill the pain."

"Cheers" is one of my favorite television shows of all time. The major characters were masterfully developed by the writers. The show was a comedy, and I'm sure the writer's goal was simply to make viewers laugh, but for me, looking at the show through my personal worldview, I saw each character trying to fill their emptiness, and the way they did it created the humor.

Norm was the large guy who sat at the end of the bar and never paid his tab. For most of the series he was happily unemployed. He was married to Vera, and his marriage was as good as the quality of time he put into it—not very much time and not very much of a marriage. He once commented to Sam that everyone in the bar lived their lives vicariously through him.

Cliff was a postman who still lived at home with his mother. He sought to fill his emptiness with facts and information by showing he knew more than everyone about everything.

Diane was a waitress who constantly reminded everyone she was really a writer waiting to make it big. She filled her emptiness with dreams of what might be.

Rebecca managed the bar for a major corporation and dreamed of being rich and successful while failing at everything she tried.

Frazier was a therapist who couldn't help himself, much less anyone else.

Sam Malone was my favorite character. He was a recovering alcoholic who ran a bar. Sam loved women, and the rest of the characters lived to hear of his conquests with women. Sam lived in the fast lane, drawing his identity from his looks, especially his hair. He loved to talk about his hair.

To me, Sam was seeking to fill the emptiness in his life through his relationships with women. While he supposedly dated many women, in truth, the character of Sam was an isolationist. He was not about to risk a real relationship, especially after Diane left the show.

Sam had been a former relief pitcher with the Red Sox. He had drank himself out of the game. Typical of the human condition, he had replaced one addiction with another. None of the addictions met Sam's deepest needs.

The desert of emptiness is a reality for all of us. We are all broken, "waiting to be mended." We all know what is feels like to "long for shelter from all that we see." It is a common experience. I believe we are born with an empty place inside our hearts, with the feeling of being separated and disconnected.

Many people, maybe all of us at times, deal with the emptiness of life with substitutes—gambling, drugs, alcohol, sex, and work are good examples. These substitutes perpetuate the problem. None of them meet the need. We understand Kris Kristofferson's lyrics, "I don't care what's right or wrong . . . help me make it through the night." The pain of emptiness hurts.

What is the source of our being in the desert of emptiness? Augustine, the great theologian of the fourth and fifth centuries, was correct when he wrote regarding God and humans, "You have created us for Yourself, and our hearts cannot be quieted until they rest in You." God created us for the purpose of having a relationship with Him, but because of sin, we are born disconnected from God.

To fill the emptiness inside us, we must enter into a relationship with God. This requires a conscious choice on our part, an acknowledgment that we are incapable of finding meaning and purpose on our own. We must choose to live as members of the family of God. We must accept the unconditional love of God and ask Him to direct our lives. Having done this, we must continually struggle to live out of that relationship and not slide back into our own efforts to save ourselves, that is, to be our own God and find our purpose in life apart from God.

Choosing to live in relationship with God gives us a new perspective. No longer are we simply seeking to please ourselves, but we notice the needs of others. We decide to be part of God's kingdom, to be part of God's work in the world. God is constantly at work seeking a relationship with all of creation, and we are to be a part of that redemptive enterprise. God is always trying to share life with us on an intimate level. He is seeking to use our experiences to draw us to Him, to involve Himself in our lives and in the lives of others.

In his book, *Sacred Journey*, Frederick Buechner describes how God used the horrible experience of his father's suicide to shape his own life.

> My father's death could have closed doors in me once and for all against the possibility of ever giving entrance to such love and thereby to such pain again. Instead, it opened up some door in me to the pain of others—not that I did much about the others, God knows, or have ever done much about them since because I am too lily-livered for that, too weak of faith, too self-absorbed and squeamish— but such pain as I had known in my own life opened up, if not my hands to help much, at least my eyes to begin seeing anyway that there is pain in every life, even the apparently luckiest, that buried griefs and hurtful memories are part of us all.[1]

Buechner found something to fill the emptiness that consumed his life after the death of his father. He began to see the world through God's eyes. He began to invest himself in others, in trying to touch the hurts of others. He would later spend his life writing, trying to touch others through his words.

Buechner found the truth that Martin Luther King, Jr. discovered when he became the leader of the civil rights movement. If you read the story of King's life, you realize he had no desire to become a famous leader. He only responded to the call of God and others. Later he would write the words that speak to the emptiness we all face. He said, "A man who will not die for something is not fit to live."

For King and others like him, the meaning of life—the answer to emptiness—came in losing themselves for the good of God and others. That is why King could say, "An individual has not started living until he can rise above the narrow confines of his individualistic concerns to the broader concerns of all humanity."

Jesus taught that the man who saves his life will lose it, but that the man who loses his life for Christ's sake will find it. Yet we spend enormous amounts of time, money, and energy trying to save our own lives from emptiness when, in reality, the emptiness would be filled if we stopped thinking about ourselves and invested our lives in God and others.

The biblical story of Zacchaeus is a familiar one to those of us who grew up going to Sunday School. I did not learn its deep meaning until much later in life. Read how Luke tells the story:

> He entered Jericho and was passing through it. A man was there named Zacchaeus; he was a chief tax collector and was rich. He was trying to see who Jesus was, but on account of the crowd he could not, because he was short in stature. So he ran ahead and climbed a sycamore tree to see him, because he was going to pass that way. When Jesus came to the place, he looked up and said to him, "Zacchaeus, hurry and come down; for I must stay at your house today." So he hurried down and was happy to welcome him. All who saw it began to grumble and said, "He has gone to be the guest of one who is a sinner." Zacchaeus stood there and said to the Lord, "Look, half of my possessions, Lord, I will give to the poor; and if I have defrauded anyone of anything, I will pay back four times as much." Then Jesus said to him, "Today salvation has come to this house, because he too is a son of Abraham. For the Son of Man came to seek out and to save the lost." (19:1-10 NIV)

The story of Zacchaeus describes a man who knew he was missing something despite his wealth. He had heard about

Jesus and wanted to see him, but as Zacchaeus sought out Jesus, Jesus was seeking out Zacchaeus. He stopped and told Zacchaeus that he wanted to go home with him, that is, to be with him. The story also reveals the unconditional acceptance of God, who received Zacchaeus as he was, a selfish, wealthy man who had probably gained his fortune through dishonesty. Notice that Jesus did not tell Zacchaeus to change his evil ways and then he would go to his house. Rather, he showed Zacchaeus acceptance and love first, and Zacchaeus responded with a changed life.

Zacchaeus found that his emptiness was met through a relationship with God and, therefore, was able to become a giver rather than a taker. Once Zacchaeus realized he was important to God, he also realized all his possessions were not so important and gave many of them away. His entire perspective on life and its meaning and purpose changed.

The desert of emptiness is never escaped by our own efforts to leave it or to fill it with experiences and possessions. We can live in the fast lane, know all the right people, take all the right pills, but the emptiness will never leave through our own efforts.

The movie *Schindler's List* is Hollywood at its best. It shows the truth of man's inhumanity to man and the reality of sin and evil. If the events in the movie were not true, I would not believe such things could happen. Yet I know my own capacity to be totally self-consumed. It is a scary reality.

The movie begins with Oskar Schindler trying to fill the emptiness of his life by trying to get rich. He is not much different from the members of the Third Reich. For Schindler, people are objects to be used at his discretion. He is a womanizer who sends his wife away rather than commit to faithfulness. The Jews are simply tools in his plan to be finally successful in business.

Something magical and wonderful happens. His eyes become open. He sees the Jews not simply as workers but as people. He finds a cause for which he is willing to die. His life takes on a totally new meaning and purpose. He is alive, possibly for the first time in his life. He becomes consumed with saving the people who work for him. Ironically, like Zacchaeus, he even gives away the money he has made, when making money had been his goal at the beginning. His goals and values totally change. His new life truly changes things. He finds his life as he gives it away. In doing this, he walks out of the desert of emptiness.

One tremendous tragedy of life is that there are needs all around us—lonely and hurting people, the homeless, the illiterate, the grief-stricken, the abused, the environment, economic justice, and racial injustice—to name a few. There is also a world full of people who wish their lives counted for something and had some larger meaning and purpose, maybe like the characters in "Cheers."

The world is full of people who allow their boredom to lead them astray. The beauty is that the desert of emptiness could become an oasis of life-giving water if only persons joined God in seeking to meet the needs of the world around them. The tragedy is that people look for love, meaning, and happiness in all the wrong places. But in losing themselves in the lives of others and in partnership with God, they would find themselves fulfilled. Even more, they would find a vision of purpose far beyond the needs of one night. They would find a tremendous thrill in being alive and out of the desert of emptiness.

Note

[1]Frederick Buechner, *The Sacred Journey* (San Francisco: Harper & Row, 1982) 56.

Chapter 10

The Desert of Hopelessness

Hopelessness is not the same thing as emptiness. It is much worse. Hopelessness is absolute and total despair. The desert of hopelessness is where you've traveled when life has no meaning or purpose, and you do not have the energy or vision to imagine a way out. It is the depths of depression. Hopelessness is wondering why you are still alive and maybe even if you want to stay alive. Hopelessness is when sadness surrounds every waking moment. I have been there, and you have probably been there, too. The desert of hopelessness is a lonely place.

The song "Turn This World Around," by Amy Grant, describes a person living in the desert of hopelessness. "The twisting road we call our lives" has left many people feeling hopeless. They are afraid to face their fears. They long for a "safe and warm place where hope can be found."

I see in the lyrics, "broken promises and dreams," a woman slumped down in a chair at the kitchen table, tears running down her face. I see hands trembling, unsure of what they are supposed to do or where they are supposed to be. I see a face that reveals shock. Her eyes have gone to a faraway place. On the table I see a telegram that reads, "We regretfully inform you that your son is missing in action." Hopelessness sets in.

- Hopelessness is powerlessness. It is wanting the world to be different and yet knowing there is nothing you can do to make it different. It is a nightmare that has become a reality and not simply a bad dream.

- Hopelessness is Mary standing at the foot of the cross and looking up at her son.

- Hopelessness is the young man in *Dead Poet's Society* who feels that his father will never allow him to be himself.

- Hopelessness is Juliet looking at Romeo and believing he is dead. Hopelessness is Romeo looking at Juliet and knowing she is dead.

- Hopelessness is the woman with the black eye and busted lip sitting at home looking at her three small children, wondering if her husband will ever stop drinking and beating her and if she can really make it on her on.

- Hopelessness is Josh Gibson and Buck Leonard who know they can hit a baseball with the best but who also know they will never get a chance to prove it because of the color of their skin.

- Hopelessness is you and me when the impossible turns out to be possible or the reality of our own evil stares us in the mirror.

- Hopelessness is the feeling of having done something we never would have done if we had been thinking clearly. It is coming face to face with our dark side and wondering if we can ever be different.

The writer of Psalm 77 was living in the desert of hopelessness when he wrote these words.

> I cry aloud to God, aloud to God, that he may hear me. In the day of my trouble I seek the Lord; in the night my hand is stretched out without wearying; my soul refuses to be comforted. I think of God, and I moan; I meditate, and my spirit faints. [Selah] You keep my eyelids from closing; I am so troubled that I cannot speak. I consider the days of old, and remember the years of long ago. I commune with my heart in the night. (vv. 1-6a)

We assume the Psalmist here was David, lamenting his problems to God following his affair with Bathsheba. By examining their story, you can understand why he wrote this psalm.

It's springtime, and David's men are fighting a war under the leadership of Joab. David remains in the palace. One night he can't sleep, so he gets up from his bed and goes walking around on his roof. While on the roof he sees a beautiful woman bathing.

At this point David is still okay. He's done nothing wrong in appreciating a beautiful woman he just happened to see bathing. Then he makes his first mistake. He sends someone to find out who she is. The report comes back that she is Bathsheba, the daughter of Eliam and the wife of Uriah. Uriah is fighting in the war. David then complicates his life further. He sends his messengers to bring her to him. She comes to him, and they sleep together. Several weeks later she sends word to David that she is pregnant. Rather than take the blame, David begins his own version of a modern-day political cover-up. He only makes matters worse.

David sends word to Joab to send Uriah home from the front to report to him. Uriah comes and reports on Joab, how the soldiers are, and how the battle is going. Then he sends Uriah home, expecting him to sleep with his wife. This way Bathsheba's pregnancy will look like the result of Uriah's trip home.

Uriah turns out to have a major personality flaw as far as David is concerned. Unlike David, at least David at this moment in his life, Uriah has integrity. He sleeps outside the palace with the other servants and doesn't go home to Bathsheba. He reasons that his fellow soldiers are sleeping in the open fields, and it would not be right for him to enjoy the pleasures of his wife while his fellow soldiers are still on the front. David hadn't counted on this.

"What a tangled web we weave," the Eagles sing in "Saturday Night." David keeps on weaving. He goes to Plan B. He tells Uriah to stay another day. He invites Uriah to dinner and gets him drunk. We all know alcohol is a great relaxer of one's inhibitions. People will do things "under the influence" they would never do clear-headed and sober. David knows this and thinks Uriah might lose a little integrity if he becomes drunk.

The plan doesn't work. Uriah still refuses to go to his house. He sleeps outside the palace. So David digs his own grave a little deeper. After Uriah returns to the front, David sends word to Joab to make sure Uriah is stationed where the battle will be the fiercest, and then pull the men back without telling Uriah so he will surely be killed. This time David's plan works. Uriah dies in battle.

In keeping with custom, Bathsheba mourns the death of her husband. Then David has her brought to the palace. She gives birth to a son. David thinks the whole thing is over. Fortunately for David, the incident is not over. I say fortunately because I believe it is not good to believe we truly get by with evil. We don't. Maybe we aren't publicly convicted or ruined, but we never really get by with anything. I say fortunately because David needs to face what he has done, deal with the hopelessness it produces in order to grow and truly reach his potential as a person and a leader.

God knows this and isn't about to let David get by without attempting to show him the truth about himself. This is the love and grace of God. God loves David enough to confront him, to push him to grow, to challenge him to be honest and thus allow the evil to have a positive result in David's life and character.

God sends the prophet Nathan to confront David. Being wise, Nathan does not just walk in and tell David what a horrible thing he has done. Rather, he tells a story:

> And the Lord sent Nathan to David. He came to him, and said to him, "There were two men in a certain city, the one rich and the other poor. The rich man had very many flocks and herds; but the poor man had nothing but one little ewe lamb, which he had bought. He brought it up, and it grew up with him and with his children; it used to eat of his meager fare, and drink from his cup, and lie in his bosom, and it was like a daughter to him. Now there came a traveler to the rich man, and he was loath to take one of his own flock or herd to prepare for the wayfarer who had come to him, but he took the poor man's lamb, and prepared that for the guest who had come to him." (2 Sam 12:1-4)

David is furious at the man in the story. He says the man deserves to die. With David's emotions at a fever pitch, Nathan calmly looks at the king and says, "You are the man!"

Now you know how David could write Psalm 77 and many other psalms with similar themes. In Psalm 13 he expresses the hopelessness that comes with realizing the depths of his own evil.

How long, Oh Lord? Will you forget me forever? How long
will you hide your face from me? How long must I bear
pain in my soul, and have sorrow in my heart all day long?
(vv. 1-2a)

The book of Psalms is a roller coaster of emotions because
David's life, like ours, is a roller coaster of good and bad, joy
and sorrow, triumph and tragedy.

I urge anyone living in the desert of hopelessness to seek a
good therapist. Many of the insights shared in this book were
gleaned from excellent counselors I have seen. Some battles
you simply can't fight alone, and I think hopelessness is one of
them. You simply can't make good decisions in the desert of
hopelessness.

Leaving the desert of hopelessness requires the courage to
open yourself emotionally to all the pain you feel. Maybe you
are in the desert because of your choices, like David's, or
because of external events such as the telegram the woman
received. Either way, healing can only occur when you
acknowledge and face your emotions.

Another option is to be open to the love and support of
others. We all have more failures than successes. If we relate to
each other out of our honesty and vulnerability, we will find
comfort from each other.

I also suggest that you be open to change. Some people
can keep on living in the same situation after tragedy; others
cannot. You may need a different home, a different job, a different situation. Such change takes courage. Sometimes it is
difficult to leave behind something, even something we know
is bad for us, because it is all we have ever known. As my
counselor, Roy Austin, once told me, "Most people will stay in
a bad relationship out of fear of having no relationship at all."
We all know of persons who stay in abusive relationships or go
back to them after leaving because the change was too
difficult.

Most importantly, be open to the power of God to heal your emotions and your soul. God meets us at our most hopeless moments. God is seeking to be with us at all times, but it seems we often do not open ourselves to God until we are desperate.

As Paul wrote in Romans 8, nothing can separate us from the love of God—not death, not stupidity, not evil, not selfishness, not tragedy. God's love is 100-percent unconditional. That means God loves us period—no ifs, ands, buts, oughts, or shoulds. God does not love us when we are good and hate us when we are bad. God cannot do that. Unconditional—no strings attached—love is the heart of God's character.

God is with us in the desert of hopelessness. He is there, ready, willing, and able to work with us in moving to a new future. He will probably use other people to help us move forward, but God will be involved.

If your hopelessness is so dark that you cannot see a glimpse of light, then your life is still not hopeless. Just ask God to help you to want to live, acknowledging that in truth, you are ambivalent about the whole thing. God can even work with that.

My college religion professor Dr. Nat Tracy used to say that the goal of Christianity is not simply to go to heaven but to have our character conformed to that of Christ. As believers, we are in the process of becoming Christlike. When we cooperate with God—that is, stay in condition to grow (with humility and a desire to learn)—we make progress. When we are stubborn and try to run our own lives, God waits patiently for the next teachable moment.

Dr. Tracy also said that most of us don't really want to become like God, to have God's kind of character. It scares us. He suggested that the best prayer for most or us is, "God help me to want to be like you."

Most of us are sad, maybe not at this moment, but deep inside us resides a little space where sadness has its permanent residence. It is the place where we try to keep the memories of terrible losses we experienced or horrendous actions we did. God lives there also, in that dark spot, ready to join us in the battle should hopelessness start to surround us. Ask God to help you want to see the light in your deepest moments of hopelessness. He will be there to guide you out of the desert of hopelessness to someplace safe and warm.

Chapter 11

The Desert of Freedom

Freedom is a wonderful thing. I love living in a country that has free elections. Okay, I admit, money may determine much of the outcome or who even runs, but I am still free to vote for the candidate I choose, whether he or she raised the most money or not.

I love the freedom to own property. My family's ranch is a treasured possession. I enjoy owning a home and a pickup truck (surely after reading this far you did not expect me to drive a car), and having the freedom to make my own decisions.

My job is about freedom. The organization I lead fights for the freedom of Baptists to follow their principles without interference from higher church bodies and conventions. I fight so that individuals will have the right to interpret Scripture for themselves and for women to have the freedom to be ministers if they feel so called of God. I fight for the freedom of others to live according to their values, even if they do not believe as I do. I am a passionate proponent of religious freedom. I fight any attempts to violate what I consider to be the separation of church and state. I fight school voucher programs, government-sponsored prayer in schools—anything that remotely smacks of coercion or lack of toleration in matters of religion.

I believe in personal freedom. I believe God loves people no matter what. I get frustrated with Christians who think they have the right to tell people how they should live and what they should believe. To my knowledge, Jesus' style was not to tell anyone what to do unless they asked. He never seemed to pass judgment unless someone asked for his opinion. The only people he condemned were the Pharisees who thought they knew it all and loved to tell people what to do.

I have always admired people who stand up for freedom. You can see from other chapters of this book that I admire Martin Luther King, Jr. I like athletes with a free spirit. I loved Joe Namath. I loved Pete Maravich. (I still cry when I see something about him on TV. I saved all the stories about him when he died.) Arnold Palmer will always be the king to me. I even liked Howard Cosell because he was the only guy who stood up for Muhammed Ali when everyone else condemned him. I respect Ali, too. A man has a right to follow his principles and shouldn't be condemned for it or stripped of his right to pursue his career. I have deep respect for Curt Flood and what he did for baseball. I believe in free agency, although I truly admire the Kirby Pucketts who show loyalty out of their freedom.

"Freeeeeedom!" I can hear Richie Havens singing now. Freedom is a wonderful thing. It is right to fight for freedom, to stand up for freedom, to urge others to believe in freedom. Love is freedom. If you love someone, you do not seek to control them. It may be proper to try to influence people, but it is never right to control in a free relationship. Loving someone means giving them freedom and respecting their actions. Love is not love if it is coerced, bought, or earned. God created us to be free. The only way to have a relationship with God is to choose freely to enter such a relationship.

So, if freedom is such a wonderful thing, why do I have a chapter on the desert of freedom? How can freedom be a desert?

Consider the story of Matt. He was a rebel, which most people loved about him. He never accepted anything at face value. He lived out of the questions of life. He was a free spirit. He would do things not because he necessarily wanted to, but because others said he shouldn't. He drove fast. He lived fast. He got kicked off the high school basketball team because he wouldn't get a haircut. He got kicked off the debate team, although he was the best debater, because he kept taking whiskey on debate trips.

Matt went to four different colleges and finally got a degree when he was 25. He just wouldn't focus on doing the work required to pass most courses. He had four jobs the first two years after college and was fired from every one. Matt wouldn't turn in sales reports, although he was a great salesman. Everybody loved doing business with him. He was a blast to be around. He was impossible to supervise.

Matt married at age 27 and divorced a year later. Spending nights alone on the road was not Matt's style. He spent his nights with other women, and this was not his wife's idea of marriage. Matt took the entire process in stride. His wife had been narrow-minded and just didn't understand freedom.

At 40 Matt still lived alone in a one-bedroom apartment. He was in construction work. It allowed him to work when he needed to and to take a break, as long as he wanted, between jobs. He still partied most nights. He was the life of the party.

Matt considered himself a free man. He had no major responsibilities, no commitments, no strings. He went where he pleased, pretty much when he pleased, and answered to no one in particular. Matt was miserably free in the desert of freedom, living with no meaningful relationships. Freedom is a desert when we misunderstand the meaning of freedom.

The song "Everything That Glitters" describes a woman who did not understand the meaning of freedom. She understood freedom as being on her own, but it cost her a relationship with her child. There is much truth in the statement "for everything you win, there's something lost." Part of maturity is having the wisdom to recognize this deep truth.

I don't know much about the actor James Dean, but I know he drove fast, lived fast, and died young. I know he supposedly was in love with Pier Angeli, one of my favorite actresses. I know my wife thinks he was handsome. (Women do love outlaws, as they say.) My guess is that James Dean misunderstood freedom, as many of us do.

Freedom is not being able to do anything you wish; that is license and leads to anarchy. Freedom is not life without any responsibilities; all of us have responsibilities. Maturity requires responsibility. Freedom is not life without any commitments; life is made up of commitments. Commitments are the bridges to trust and meaningful relationships with others. Freedom is not life without limits; all of us are limited by our humanity, intelligence, and gifts. I can't fly. I can't multiply 456,789 times 874,338 without time or a calculator (preferably the latter). I can't play professional football at 160 pounds with 5.1, 40-yard-dash speed. I am limited.

Dr. Nat Tracy defined freedom as "glad obedience to authority." Now before you react negatively to that definition, allow me to explain it further. I share many people's reactions to authority.

I love the scene in the movie *Annie Hall* when Woody Allen is trying to drive and runs into three or four cars. The police come. Woody gets out of the car, takes out his driver's license, and tears it up. Then he tells the cop, "It's not your fault. I just have have this problem with authority." Believe me, I understand.

Authority can be abusive. I admire Martin Luther King, Jr. for standing up to Bull Conner in Alabama. I admire the apostles standing up to the authorities in order to preach the gospel as recorded in the book of Acts. There are times when we must reject authority out of principle.

Authority is often good and necessary. The fact is that everyone of us lives under authority. There is the authority of gravity. Jump off a skyscraper, and you will fall and probably die. The freedom to live depends on being obedient to that authority.

The freedom to drive from Dallas to San Antonio safely depends on your willingness to be obedient to authority. If you insist on exercising your freedom to drive on the wrong side of the road, you will not arrive safely. You will probably be killed and kill someone else in the process.

Music demands obedience to authority. When I sit down at the piano, I only have the freedom to make noise. I do not know the rules of melody or which keys to hit to make music rather than noise. Stevie Wonder can sit at the piano and, if he is obedient to the rules that govern how a piano works, make the beautiful sounds we hear in all his great songs.

I do play the guitar. You can't necessarily go from a G to B7 to C#ᵐ and get music. You'll probably just get noise. You can play in the key of G or C or D and do variations of these keys, but you can't combine two keys at the same time. There are rules to follow.

I am not a "rules and regulations" Christian. I don't believe Jesus was into rules and regulations. Yet it is important to be obedient to Christ if we are to grow as Christians. How can you practice obedience and not be a "rules and regulations" Christian?

The answer lies in the word "glad." The Pharisees in Scripture were into rules and regulations. They were not into relationships. God desires a relationship. True Christians gladly seek to be obedient to Christ. Christ's teachings are not about rules, but about principles. Dr. Tracy called them "principles of health."

For example, one should not refrain from committing adultery simply because adultery breaks God's law. Not committing adultery also allows a marriage to have a chance. One should not commit murder not just because it is wrong, but because it also allows humanity to survive. Violence always leads to violence. One should not refuse to steal just because it is wrong, but because of respect for others and their possessions. Society without respect for others results in violent expressions. When you study the commandments of God, you realize they all are based on common sense for the common good. Obedience to them is for our own good. It sets us free.

Freedom is always within the context of limits. We can take it to the limit, but if we go beyond the limit, there is a price to pay. Freedom, defined as being able to do anything you want, is truly just somebody talking and talking nonsense. If you are looking for that kind of freedom, you won't be able to find it. You are looking in the wrong place.

The freedom to receive an academic degree requires that you meet certain standards. Many scholarships require maintaining a certain grade point average. The freedom to have a growing marriage means that you honor certain restrictions and work hard at building a relationship. The freedom to hold a job means that you meet certain expectations in terms of time or production or both.

True freedom, in a Christian context, is gladly being obedient to God's commandments because you have experienced God relationally. You know God as good. You know He wants what is best for you. True obedience is not given in order for

God to love you—He already does. Obedience is given out of gratitude for all God has done for you, out of trust in the relationship. Obedience trusts that following God is the best way to live. Obedience leads to a fulfilled life.

Obedience is not easy. It is not the blind application of rules or laws to specific problems. You do need the wisdom to apply God's commandments wisely out of your freedom. Different circumstances call for different applications.

For example, I believe divorce is always a sin. I also believe a person should not have to live in an abusive relationship. I believe war is wrong, that killing is wrong. I also believe Hitler should not have been allowed to achieve his goals of world domination. Often our choices are between two evils. Life is difficult. Easy answers seldom work in the real world. We have the freedom to make the best choices we can, always seeking God's will in the midst of the situation and seeking to respond faithfully.

True freedom may mean being disobedient to a lower authority in order to honor a higher authority. This is civil disobedience as advocated by Henry David Thoreau and Martin Luther King, Jr. Both also advocated respectfully paying the price for disobedience in order to produce the most good.

The greater truth is that commitments increase freedom. Commitment to another makes marriage possible. Commitment to family makes emotionally and physically healthy children possible. Commitment to fiscal responsibility makes it possible to own a home, take a vacation, and maybe buy a new pickup truck. Commitment to a cause or to principles makes societal change possible. Commitments set us free to achieve, produce, and succeed. Commitment to Christ makes a meaningful life more possible along with eternity in relationship with God. Commitments open the doors of freedom in real ways. We are free to commit to God and His values, to common sense, and to the principles of health. Making these commitments enables us to discover true freedom.

Matt never learned this lesson. He was so free, he ended up having nothing. The truth unseen by Matt is that our commitments, responsibilities, and relationships give our lives meaning. Matt never became an adult or accepted the responsibilities that go with maturity. In truth, he became imprisoned, not by his desire for freedom, but by his resistance to limits.

Jesus said the truth would make us free. What truths do we need to know to be free? Here are a few suggestions:

- We are created in the image of God and for relationship with God. We will never be who we were created to be without submission to God's authority. God made us and desires what is best for our lives. Accept God's authority. Set yourself free from searching for the meaning of life.

- We are important and valuable because God says so. We do not earn worth from success, society, or the opinions of others. Set yourself free from the need for approval of others.

- We are able to reach our potential as persons and have productive lives only in relationship with our Creator. Set yourself free from earning your salvation.

- We are to be partners with God in His effort to love the world and bring all into the family of God. Set yourself free from searching for a purpose in life.

- We are God's ambassadors in the fight against evil and its manifestations—greed, racism, abuse of power, abuse of the earth and other persons, and selfishness—to name only a few of the things we battle. Set yourself free to serve rather than rule.

Glad obedience to the authority of Christ unleashes the power of God in your life. It sets you free to live the most meaningful and exciting life possible, the life you were created to live.

Freedom is a wonderful thing. True freedom comes from choosing wisely who and what you will serve—your own selfish desires or the God who created you. That choice will determine if you are truly free or stuck in the desert of freedom.

Chapter 12

Out of the Desert

I learned to play the guitar in college. My talent for music is limited, and my talent for singing is nonexistent. Bubba (Jim to the rest of the world that knows him) is my guitar-playing partner from college and still is today. Bubba says I'm tone deaf. Still, I try. He's definitely the better performer of the Bubba Brothers, although I write all our songs. At least I contribute something.

One of first songs I learned to play on the guitar was Neil Young's "Needle and the Damage Done." Young's song is a mournful ballad about life in a desert of despair, the dangers of drug abuse. "Peaceful Easy Feeling" was another of the first songs I learned to play. This song, in contrast, is about a person feeling secure and confident in a loving relationship.

If writer Scott Peck is correct and "life is difficult," then how do we keep our feet on the ground? How do we survive the deserts that seek to destroy us? How can we live with a "peaceful, easy feeling," despite the fact that there is a little junkie in all of us? We all struggle with our demons. Let me give you a few suggestions for surviving the dark, desert highway of life and having peace in your life.

(1) *Have a realistic view of life.* You can't avoid all the deserts described in this book. Genesis tells the story. Human beings sought to be God rather than live in relationship with God. The Bible calls it "sin." The newspaper reports daily on the reality of evil and sin.

I still believe life is wonderful, and the world is a great place, but I am realistic about the nature of life and people. Bad things are going to happen to me and to those I love. Not all my dreams will come true. Some of my decisions will be bad ones. But in the midst of it all, I hope to have a "peaceful easy feeling" most of the time and keep my feet planted solidly on the ground. One of the defense mechanisms I use to protect myself is my mother's advice to "live in the real world." We often set ourselves up for failure and disappointment by having an unrealistic view of life.

We've all known people so desperate for love that every time they meet someone new, they are convinced they have found the person of their dreams, even after only knowing them a week. Every new relationship is the love of their lives!

We've all known people so desperate to get rich that every deal is a good deal. They never exercise critical thinking in examining a new opportunity. Every opportunity is the real thing, the deal of a lifetime.

All of life is bittersweet. All persons have positive and negative qualities. Every relationship takes work and is sometimes heavenly, sometimes hellish, and often a little of both. Having your feet planted on the ground with a realistic worldview is very helpful in surviving the deserts of life. It can help you have peace in the midst of many of life's storms.

(2) *Have a realistic view of yourself.* Remember the saying, "You are very important to be so insignificant." There are more than 6 billion people in the world, and that can make you feel rather insignificant. You are one of the people in the world. That makes you pretty important, especially to the part of the world that knows your name, loves your face, rejoices in your presence, and shares life with you.

Lance and Chad Currie may be insignificant to most readers, but they're very important to me. They are my sons. What happens to them, what they do, how they live, what they believe—everything about them is important to me. I love them. I treasure them. I hurt when they hurt. I rejoice when they are happy. They are a great part of my life and are more important to me than I have words to describe. Hopefully, you are that important to another person; certainly, you are that important to God.

You are also human, which means you will live part of your life on the dark, desert highway and have a tremendous capacity to act in evil ways. You do have your demons and desires. You will make mistakes and bad choices. Sometimes you will be downright mean and selfish in ways even you can't believe. When you do live out of your darkness, you will be lost in the desert for awhile, lost on a dark, desert highway. When you realize it, remember God's grace and unconditional love. Tell yourself you are too important and special to live so selfishly. Remind yourself that God and others think a great deal of you. Remind yourself that you have gifts to give the world, needs you can meet, joys you can share.

It is important to have a positive feeling about yourself. It is wise to have a healthy, realistic self-image. No, you are not a perfect person, but you are a worthwhile person. Make peace with your dark side. Accept the bittersweet reality of your own character. Allow God to do in you what you cannot do yourself.

(3) *Have a realistic view of God.* God is love. God, through the Holy Spirit, dwells in the life of every believer. God seeks to have a personal relationship with each of us. But God is not a magician. God does not run our lives by making decisions for us. God does not interfere in human decision making. God does not protect us from pain in our lives. Nor does God make every business deal and marriage work, every child healthy, everyone live at peace, or keep us all from getting stuck on the dark, desert highways of life.

Much disappointment comes from an unrealistic understanding of what it means to be a Christian, a follower of Christ and his teachings. Sometimes we believe or are taught that if we just give our lives to God, all our problems will disappear. Nothing could be farther from the truth. In fact, following Christ will probably open a whole new set of problems.

We live in a world that does not value God. Therefore, when we make the decision to value God, it creates conflict in ourselves and our relationships. A Christian should have a different view of business than someone living only for themselves. A Christian should have a different view of sexuality than just whatever feels good. A Christian should have a different understanding of power and leadership. Being a servant in a world that values power and prestige is difficult.

Being a Christian means we share our lives with God and have made a conscious commitment to attempt to adopt the values of God. We try to see the worth of all persons, of all creation. We seek to demonstrate God's love to the people we encounter. We seek to view situations and life from God's perspective with God's redemptive purpose in mind.

God walks with us along the dark, desert highways and seeks to help us avoid the choices that bring us to the deserts. God is the light to guide us through the darkness. God is always with us, but does not supernaturally protect us from the deserts. It is often in the desert that we are most teachable, most open to learning the lessons God can teach us through life's experiences.

Remember that the goal of God in your life is to make you like Himself. Becoming Christlike is a process, not magic. It is not something that happens immediately when you open yourself up to God and His love and power. It is a journey that will last all of your life and all of eternity. Since God is inexhaustible, we will never become totally like Him. The excitement is the journey.

(4) *Learn to be honest.* Honesty is an absolute necessity to survive the dark, desert highway. No one grows without realizing their need for growth. No one is cured of cancer who refuses to admit they have cancer and then submit to treatment. The first step toward healing is admitting the disease. The second step is asking for help.

I love a paragraph early in Walker Percy's novel, *Love in the Ruins.* Maybe it is because I recognize myself in it. Maybe you will recognize yourself.

> I, for example, am a Roman Catholic, albeit a bad one. I believe in the Holy Catholic Apostolic and Roman Church, in God the Father, in the election of the Jews, in Jesus Christ His Son our Lord, who founded the Church on Peter his first vicar, which will last until the end of the world. Some years ago, however, I stopped eating Christ in Communion, stopped going to mass, and have since fallen into a disorderly life. I believe in God and the whole business, but I love women best, music and science next, whiskey next, God fourth, and my fellowman hardly at all. Generally I do as I please. A man, wrote John, who says he believes in God and does not keep his commandments is a liar. If John is right, then I am a liar. Nevertheless, I still believe.[1]

I love the honesty of that paragraph. I believe it describes some of the incongruencies in our lives. We love God and want to do right, but our values and priorities are mixed up. We are all liars, but we still believe—and God loves us anyway.

If the best you can do right now is honestly tell God that He is fourth on your priority list, then tell Him. Shoot straight. Ask God to give you the desire to live totally for Him, even if for brief moments at a time. God can work with that. That's all He had to work with in the Bible—people like Noah, who got drunk and laid around naked; Moses, who had an anger problem; Jacob, the trickster; Samson, the womanizer; David, the adulterer; Jeremiah, the moaner; and Peter, James, John, and the other disciples who spent part of their time so self-centered that they argued among themselves about who was the most important.

(5) *Learn to let go.* Sometimes the only option we have in life is to leave it alone, let it go. There is nothing we can do about it. Whatever it is—a broken relationship, a shattered dream—it's over and done with. We can't fix it by deception, pride, living in isolation, playing the victim, or getting angry and staying angry. There is nothing that will fix it like it used to be, whatever *it* is.

Maybe, with God, we can learn something from the experience. Possibly something good can come from the experience, but nothing can fix it and make it like it used to be. Our hope is that something new can be made from it—maybe even a wiser, more loving, more tolerant, more understanding new you. You have to let go in order to open up the possibility of growth and change.

Holding on to your old prejudices, excuses, and crutches will never allow you to change. The painful work of growth as a person requires letting go—risking—being willing to go into the unknown. Peace often comes when we let go—let go of the past, the memory that holds us, the dream that will never become a reality, the way it used to be, our poor self-image.

(6) *Learn to be still.* The song "Learn To Be Still," mentioned in the introduction, is beautiful, almost like a prayer. The advice it gives is inspired.

Learn to be still. Why? Because you can't know yourself without spending time with yourself. You can't know God without spending time with God. It is in the stillness that we are able to be realistic, honest, open, and can let go of our fears, disappointments, and hurts. A person who knows himself and what he believes is less likely to follow "one more starry-eyed messiah," as the lyrics say, instead of the true and living God.

Learn to be still. Why? Because a person who cannot tolerate being alone is not healthy. People who have to be with others are possessive, jealous in relationships, and lack self-esteem. They are clingy in relationships and dependent. They will sacrifice their values to be loved and accepted.

Learn to be still. Why? Because when you are still, you can silence the voices in your head with sound reasoning. You are more likely to avoid living out the lyric of "wondering in the desert and following the wrong gods home."

Jesus constantly went away to be alone with the Father. He went away to be still, to reflect, to pray, to question, and even to struggle. At one point he prayed, "If it is possible, let this cup pass from me; yet not what I want but what you want."

Jesus started his ministry with stillness. He went away and fasted for 40 days and nights. He ended his ministry in stillness, praying in the garden. It is in the stillness that we hear his still, small voice. It is in the stillness that the pressures of life are lifted. It is in the stillness that we see reality, away from the hurriedness of daily survival.

(7) *Invest your life in service.* I did not know Princess Diana, nor do I know much about her life. I thought she was physically beautiful and seemed to carry herself with great class. She seemed to care about people. The rewritten version of the song "Candle in the Wind," which Elton John sang at Princess Diana's funeral, is one of the most beautiful songs I have ever heard. The lyrics are especially inspiring, particularly the line, "You were the grace that placed itself where lives were torn apart."

What an incredible description of the way a Christian's life should be. We are all called to place ourselves where lives are torn apart. We are called to be Jesus to a hurting world. When we do this, we find that something magical happens. Our life has meaning and purpose. We tend to leave the deserts behind us. Life is bigger than our personal struggles. We find peace and contentment. As Jesus said, "For whoever wants to save his life will lose it, but whoever loses his life for me will find it" (Matt 16:25). And how do we "lose our life" for Jesus? By being "the grace that placed itself where lives are torn apart."

The closer we walk with Christ, the more we will avoid the deserts of life. My prayer is that you will open your heart to God and allow Him to use this book to comfort your soul on the dark, desert highways of life. God bless you on your journey.

> Bless the Lord, O my soul, and all that is within me, bless his holy name. Bless the Lord O my soul, and do not forget all his benefits—who forgives all your iniquity, who heals all your diseases, who redeems your life from the Pit, who crowns you with steadfast love and mercy, who satisfies you with good as long as you live so that your youth is renewed like the eagle's.
>
> The Lord works vindication and justice for all who are oppressed. He made known his ways to Moses, his acts to the people of Israel. The Lord is merciful and gracious, slow to anger and abounding in steadfast love. He will not always accuse, nor will he keep his anger forever. He does not deal with us according to our sins, nor repay us according to our iniquities. For as the heavens are high above the earth, so great is his steadfast love toward those who fear him; as far as the east is from the west, so far he removes our transgressions from us. (Ps 103:1-12)

Note

[1]Walker Percy, *Love in the Ruins* (New York: Farrar, Strauss, & Giroux, 1971) 6.